Nitish is a young man with a mission. Through his brilliant travelogues and scholarly historical pieces, he aims to spread a mix of nostalgia, a feeling of wonder and an enchanted vision. Inherent in his labour is a sense of innate pride and purposeful intent. The one word that defines his writing? Inspiring!

Mrutyunjay Sarangi, IAS(Rtd)
Eminent writer and poet. Editor of LiteraryVibes, a popular monthly eMagazine; formerly a Secretary to the Government of India and a Judge of a Tribunal

---

When one goes in search of the bright spots on the globe and discovers a few fantastic people, places and events he possibly becomes a Nitish Nivedan Barik feeling like sharing his finds with others. Be that the Anger Olympics at Tokyo or the Homewood Middle School experience in the US; People like Dr Kotnis or Mihir Sen; Places like Rwanda or Auroville. This slim book carries heavy doses in a strip of mere thirty capsules and offers a nice and healthy reading. The narratives are at once engrossing and enlightening both.

Dash Benhur, Celebrated Odia writer
Academician and Columnist, Recipient of Odisha Sahitya Akademi Award and Central Sahitya Akademi Bal Puraskar

---

Brilliantly written, the essays of Nitish Nivedan Barik unfolds myriad ideas about socio-cultural life of our country. The book presents before us a young mind who is equally excited and perturbed with developments around him. For him, the whole world is one family and any development in the field of nature, environment, sports, culture, politics, or economy affects him. An excellent work of a promising wordsmith which is unputdownable.

- Gourahari Das, Distinguished Odia Writer
Editor, columnist, and a Sahitya Akademi Award Winner

Nitish Nivedan Barik is a brilliant storyteller. His stories are based on various life experiences. For example, his stories of multiple athletes competing in different sports events, including the Olympics are breathtaking. They are accurate in their descriptions and delightfully presented. Every sports fan will enjoy reading them.

Annapurna Devi Pandey,
Renowned Scholar, Writer, Filmmaker, and Educator; Currently Teaching at the University of California, Santa Cruz, USA

"Leaves from History" by Nitish is an inspiring and enlightening collection. This assemblage of anecdotes, significant and varied historical events, and personalities, drawn from different times and climes, enriched with his field experiences and presented in a lucid manner, is sure to captivate and refresh readers.

Digambar Mishra, Former Professor and Chair,
Division of Social Sciences, Miles College, AL, USA

Leaves from History

Nitish Nivedan Barik

BLACK EAGLE BOOKS
Dublin, USA | Bhubaneswar, India

Black Eagle Books
USA address:
7464 Wisdom Lane
Dublin, OH 43016

India address:
E/312, Trident Galaxy, Kalinga Nagar,
Bhubaneswar-751003, Odisha, India

E-mail: info@blackeaglebooks.org
Website: www.blackeaglebooks.org

First International Edition Published by
Black Eagle Books, 2024

LEAVES FROM HISTORY
by **Nitish Nivedan Barik**

Copyright © Nitish Nivedan Barik

All rights reserved. No part of this publication may be reproduced, stored in a retrieval system, or transmitted, in any form or by any means, electronic, mechanical, photocopying, recording or otherwise without the prior permission of the publisher.

Cover & Interior Design: Ezy's Publication

ISBN- 978-1-64560-618-5 (Paperback)
Library of Congress Control Number: 2024950927

Printed in the United States of America

Dedicated to
My loving parents
Prof Niranjan Barik and
Smt Kiranmayee Mohapatra

Acknowledgement

It gives me immense pleasure to announce that my first book," Leaves from History" which I have been planning for so long, is finally going to see the light of the day. I owe a great debt of gratitude to many people.

First and foremost, I would like to thank my family members for their unwavering support throughout this literary journey. To my dad, Prof. Niranjan Barik, thank you for instilling in me the values of hard work and perseverance, and for encouraging me to read, write, and publish. Your wisdom and encouragement have been a constant source of inspiration, leading to my writings taking the form of this book.

To my mom, Kiran Mohapatra, who has been my biggest cheerleader—thank you for your endless love, understanding, and patience. Your belief in me has given me the courage to pursue my professional and literary dreams.

My sincere gratitude goes to my paternal uncles, Dr. Srikanta Barik and Dr. Sudarshan Barik, and my Piusa, Mr. Bhaskar Chandra Biswal, for their unwavering love, affection, and encouraging words after reading my stories, published from time to time.

To my wonderful sisters, Upali and Ananya, and my brothers-in-law, Ritesh and Biplab—your constant support and encouragement have been invaluable. You have been my sounding boards, my supporters, and my motivators. I am forever grateful to have you by my side.

Sincere thanks to Professor Digambar Mishra and Auntie Professor Josna Mishra, both formerly of Miles College, Birmingham, AL, USA for constantly encouraging me from across the shore (America) and reading my stories on Facebook and Literary Vibes.

My special thanks to Dr. Mrutyunjay Sarangi for providing me a platform through Literary Vibes to publish my articles, which I have compiled into this book.

This book wouldn't have been possible without each of you. Thank you for being my foundation and my inspiration.

Again ,for their blurbs, I am indebted to Dr. Mrutyunjay Sarangi, Dash Benhur (Dr. Jitendra Narayan Dash), Dr. Gourahari Das, Professor Annapurna Devi Pandey, and Professor Digambar Mishra for taking the time to read my scripts and provide their comments.

Finally ,my sincere thanks to my international publisher, Black Eagle Books, especially Mr. Satya Patnaik and Mr. Ashok Parida, for the effort they put into publishing this book on short notice.

Nitish Nivedan Barik

Contents

A Young Man Who Made History - Marvan Attapatu	11
On Olympic Spirit, The Spirit of Positive Vibes	15
One Family, One Nation and One Country	21
Umuganda As Patriotic Agenda with Cow As the Key To Discord and Accord	26
A Small Country Playing A Big Role on the World Stage	33
Letters From A Father to A Son	38
A Towering Man on A Towering Tower	45
Sri Aurobindo, The Great Nationalist And The Lover of Humanity	49
A School Away From A School (My Days In An American School)	54
About A Historical Man and A Historical City	59
About A Monument That Swears in The Name Of Democracy	65
The Story Of Singapore and Lee Kuan Yew as A Unique Leader!	68
Some Glimpses From 1942 Quit India Movement: Daring Women & Children Who Lived or Died With or For the Flag	76
Story of A Tree That Led To A Township - A Project Of Human Unity	82
About A Friend Of India, Also The Friend Of The Poor & Downtrodden!	90
My Mcg Moment	95
The Story of an Indian Hero on the Battlefronts in China	103
About Some Black Swan Events!	108
About the Man Born With Large Head and Big Ears	113
A Resilient Boy Who Turned Adversity into Opportunity!	117
A Man Of The Earth	121
The Vaikom Movement	125
A Solo Adventurer in the Seas & Oceans	131
The Man Who Became the First To Set Foot on Top of The World	134
An Encounter That Happened A Hundred Years Back	141
An Iconic Bridge	146
An Iron Lady Of India As An Inspiration to Everyone	151
A Revolution and The Symbolic Role of Flowers	157
A Healing Statesman	161
Atomic Thoughts about the Little Boy and Fat Man!	165

A Young Man Who Made History - Marvan Attapatu

The leaf is from Cricket history. Cricket, like any other game, has many surprises and lessons to impart. We learn how to keep calm in an adverse situation from M.S.Dhoni for which he is well-known as Mr. Cool. Channelizing anger, one may learn from Dada (Sourav Ganguly) or from a roaring Kohli. Similarly, the lesson not to give up in the face of ignominious failure, also we get from Cricket! Attapatu in our neighbourhood, Sri Lanka is the stunning example of the latter.

Marvan Attapatu made his debut as a 20 year old lad in Test cricket for Sri Lanka in 1990; he scored a duck in his first innings. And again, in his second innings he crashed with a zero on the score board.

He was dropped from the team whereupon he went back to the nets for more practice. He played more first-class cricket where he made impressive scores. The wait was not too long. Just after 2 years he was called upon to show his mettle in Sri Lanka's international cricket. This time, he had already put in rigorous effort and practices at

the net. But lo, his scores unfortunately were zero again in the first innings and just one in the following one!

Not surprisingly he was dropped again. Attapatu did go back to the domestic cricket where he impressed the onlookers and selectors by scoring tons. The runs, though huge, were not perhaps adequate to wash away his great pain and trauma he would have suffered for his blatant failures in the past internationals. Well, seventeen months later, opportunity knocked on his door again. Marvan got to bat in both innings of the Test. But look, his scores were a pair of zeros. What a bad luck for the budding talent!

At that time, his average was 0.16, 1 run and five ducks under his belt. In such backdrop, would the selectors ever think of giving him another chance? It was said that he lacked the big-match temperament, and his technique was not up to mark at the highest level. He would have naturally pondered what went so wrong with him at international level. Undeterred, Marvan never stopped aspiring and trying.

Three years later, another chance came on his way, thanks to the selectors for having faith in his talent. This time, he rose to the occasion and did not prove the selectors wrong. He came extraordinarily brilliant, Marvan Samson Atapattu wrote his illustrious career, thereafter, scoring over five thousand runs for the country which included sixteen centuries and six double hundreds. And more significantly and deservingly he went on to captain his country. All this despite taking over six years to score his second run in Test cricket. The trajectory is bound to surprise many. The table had turned, and Attapatu was now described as one of the most technically adroit batsmen of his time.

It is a lesson to learn from Attapatu how to handle failure and never to lose heart but bounce back to victory with perseverance and determination, keeping your cool by leaving the nightmarish failures buried in the past. Attapatu's struggle was for six years of trying, and failing. In a situation of steady iconic failures anybody in his place would have been tempted to give up, try another career or seek a switch over of his passion from cricket to something else. Or he could have just remained satisfied limiting his interest to playing a club or county cricket if possible. Or as said the easiest would have been for him just to give up. But he was great at heart not to give up. That made history. Atapattu mesmerised the people with his knocks that rolled into centuries. One could say that when he was on a song, he brought everyone else alongside with him. He has the record of scoring centuries against all Test-playing nations.

When failure or rejection stares somebody on the face he or she should think of Attapatu. By not giving up, and rather believing in yourself you can hitch your wagon to a star. If you stick to your gun, the run will automatically come. You could even rise to be a captain of the game or leader of the enterprise someday. So, the young people must take a leaf from Attapatu's life history, never to give up so easily even when failure hurts you so much!

In an interview to the Indian newspaper, The Hindu in 2020, Attapatu said how 'Attitude' is very important. "You have got to have that attitude where you are ready to improve yourself every day. It is a learning curve for everybody, be it a batsman or a bowler. You need to keep that in mind. You need to learn something new every day," the 'Zero to Hero' had said.

On Olympic Spirit, the Spirit of Positive Vibes

2020 Tokyo Olympic held in 2021 would go down in history as "COVID Olympics" or the "Pandemic Olympics". It has also been called the "Anger Olympics.", as many Japanese were upset that their country was hosting such a mega risky event in the middle of the global pandemic to which they cannot be direct witnesses in physical mode while Tokyo itself remained in a COVID-19 state-of-emergency. Many people in the outside world were truly surprised that it happened at all. At the end of the day, yes, it was the US, like many other times in the past got at the top of the table with 39 golds,41 Silvers and 33 Bronze making an impressive total of 113 medals closely followed by China that bagged 38 gold 32 Silver and 18 Bronze with a tally of 88. The host country came third with 27,14 and 17 respectively which added up to a respectable fifty-eight. India recorded its best as it jumped to 47th rank in the medal tally after Neeraj Chopra won the gold in Javelin.

With a total of seven medals at Tokyo India surpassed its 2012 record in London. While Syria, a very small country, was placed in the 86th position with a mere one bronze, Pakistan, India's arch rival failed to bag even a single medal in this Olympic and was therefore nowhere in the medal list. Significantly, some of the other neighbouring countries of India – Sri Lanka, Bangladesh, and Nepal also drew blank and failed to make it to the tally as even they didn't win a single medal. But are these statistics everything in the Olympic? No, it is the Olympic spirit!

The Olympic spirit is basically to take part irrespective of your win or failure. The Olympic spirit is best expressed in the Olympic Creed: The most important thing in the Olympic Games is not to win but to take part, just as the most important thing in life is not the triumph but the struggle. The essential thing is not to have conquered but to have fought well.

Two events in Tokyo this year brought out the Olympic spirit in the best ways possible. First it is about USA's Isaiah Jewett and Botswana's Nijel Amos in the 800m semi-final. Jewett was almost coming third, close to close with Amos following behind with a razor margin difference when both of them fell down on the track a few meters from the finishing line. Jewett later said in an interview that 'it felt as if he had been hit in the back of his heel, which threw off his stride and caused his legs to tangle.' Those who would have watched it live on the field or on small screens would have been amazed to see the Olympic spirit live – they did not exhibit even an iota of hurt, anger or hard feelings ! Rather just the opposite. Both these runners were good sports. The two helped each other to their feet, put their arms around each other and resumed the run to finish the race in that semifinal heat, just 54 seconds behind the winner. It has been hailed as a remarkable show of sportsmanship. Amos stepped back to give Jewett a one-stride lead, with Jewett finishing second-to-last at 2:38.12 and Amos last at 2:38.49.

A bend on the road is not the end of the journey. Two great examples we may cite from Tokyo Olympic 2020 in this short paragraph.US star gymnast Simone Biles, 24, had cherished a career haul of nine Olympic golds, perhaps to reenact the record set by Soviet gymnast Larisa Latynina in Tokyo in 1964 and many also hoped so. Unfortunately, on July 27, Biles dropped out of the women's gymnastics team final after one disappointing vault, saying she had to take care of her mental health. She then excused herself from four out of five individual events, citing the "twisties," which refers to a condition where gymnasts suffer from a loss of perceptual awareness of body positioning during a spin in mid-air. Interestingly Biles didn't entirely miss her chance to be in the record book in Tokyo. She did return and register a victory with a bronze on the balance beam, adding to the silver she had helped win in the team event despite her early departure. Sifan Hassan, a long-distance runner of Netherlands, stumbled on the ground just when she was powering through the last lap of the women's 1,500-meter heat. As it is reported a runner ahead of her had tripped, prompting a domino effect on her. Hassan it is said tried and failed to jump over a fallen runner but then fell down herself. But from the nightmarish even the most incredible thing happened. Sifan was undeterred; she immediately got back up and, now suddenly from the last place, raced to pass eleven runners to finish first for her spectacular golden moment. It was a fantastic comeback. To add another feather to her cap and that of her country, she went on to win gold in the women's 5,000-meter race too that same day, becoming the first Dutch woman to medal in a long-distance race.

Olympic spirit and unity can never be an empty

slogan. The 'Olympic spirit is alive and well' was once again displayed in the joy of Italy's Gianmarco Tamberi and Qatar's Mutaz Essa Barshim as they were leaping up and down and embracing each other in the Olympic Stadium. Both had agreed to tie for a gold medal rather than deciding the winner in a jump-off. In 2016, just before the Rio Olympics, Tamberi had suffered a serious injury while attempting a 2.41-metre high jump.

Round after round, the two star athletes had simply failed to outdo one another — prompting an official to tell them the next step was a "jump-off," to see who could simply outlast the other. As the official went to ask the two athletes about the jump-off, Barshim, the reigning world champion in the event instead asked, "Can we have two golds?" to which official had instantly said, " It is possible, yes." This led the two athletes to jump up in joy and hug each other. People called it the best Olympic moment and saw tears of joy all around the stadium and on Twitter- it became a symbol of the sportsmanship and friendship the Olympics were designed to create.

Every Olympic has its share of positive vibes – the Olympic Spirit in action that makes the spirit of any onlooker or observer soar sky high. It brings to mind a leaf from history – from 1936 German Olympic. It is about African-American athlete Jesse Owens who stole the show in the face of many odds and challenges. Those who know about Fascism or Nazism know how racism is heart of that ideology. The 1936 Olympic Games were part of Nazi leader Adolf Hitler's grand plan to prove Aryan superiority. But Owen exploded the myth of Aryan supremacy by winning four gold medals. Owens came out at the top in the 100m in 10.30 seconds, the 200m in 20.70 seconds, and then the long jump, with an impressive leap of 8.06 metres. The fourth gold for him came in the 4x100m relay, in which Owens had formed a key part of the team that set a new world record of 39.80 seconds. By the way Owens had set a record that would stand for 48 years before being broken by compatriot Carl Lewis at the 1984 Olympics.

Interestingly, his gold in the long jump came apparently after getting some valuable and timely advice about his run-up from a German competitor, Luz Long. This piece of advice helped Owens reach the final after a couple of failed attempts. As it turned out, Owens had set a new Olympic record (8.06m) leaving Long for the second position to grab silver (7.87m). This would have dismayed the hyper-national crowd in Berlin, including Hitler, by what they saw, but Long wasn't. To the surprise of many and the credit of the German, Long was the first to congratulate Owens and later walked around the stadium, arm-in-arm with the later. The duo even posed together for pictures.

As Owens would record later, "It took a lot of courage for him to befriend me in front of Hitler." Perhaps for History to record and treasure it for all time to come he had said the golden words, "You can melt down all the medals and cups I have and they wouldn't be plating on the 24-carat friendship I felt for Luz Long at that moment. "All will agree that it was a friendship Luz Long, Jesse Owens (a White and a Black respectively) had woven that triumphed over racism and would be a lesson for humanity. The story of Owens and Long's friendship has been commented as great demonstration of the fact how sports could unite people across gender, race and nationalities, even in the toughest circumstances.

Ironically, the hero of 1936 Berlin Olympics did not get a White House invitation nor reception that he deserved. It is said because he was the grandson of slaves, Owens was snubbed by his own president when Franklin D. Roosevelt failed to greet him, an honour and custom for returning Olympic champions to the home country. See how Indian Prime Minister Narendra Modi had received the Indian Tokyo Olympic winners and participants at a breakfast meet and talking to all of them individually and collectively. Though not fully, yet a lot has changed in America. Racism, casteism, misogyny are still structurally ingrained in many societies. The recent Taliban takeover of Kabul cast a shadow over the aspirations of Afghan women. Many wondered if Afghanistan would be able to send a women's contingent to the 2024 Paris Olympics. However, as a testament to the resilience of Afghan women, a gender-balanced team was indeed sent. In contrast, American women shone brightly at the Tokyo Olympics, with nearly 60% of the U.S. medalists being women. Let us hope the spirit of sportsmanship prevails everywhere – the spirit of friendship, brotherhood, humanity, and cosmopolitan culture. May the Olympic spirit, with its positive vibes, spread beyond isolated stadiums to the entire world stage, where we all play our part with a sportsman's spirit.

(Sources and stories are many, but the spirit is one)

One Family, One Nation and One Country

The title of this story may sound funny and strange. "Principality of Hutt River" if searched in Google, will show it to be a self-proclaimed tiny sovereign state, but not recognized by any, attracting many tourists from all over the world till the other day. It had caught international attention for about half a century.

Only seventy-five square kilometre in area, it is a micro-nation inside the Australian continent and is approximately 500 km from Perth. Visa was needed to visit the small picturesque country, which was however available on arrival for a price of just four dollars on production of your valid passport at their government office–cum-reception. Somebody from their so-called royal family was certainly there to welcome and show you courtesy while stamping visa and narrating the history and geography of the special State.

Leonard Casley who gave himself the title of a Prince and declared himself as Sovereign of this land was the founder of this country in 1970. Well, one can be a sovereign with a prefix of Prince to one's name, the current glaring example being that of Prince Mohammed bin Salman, the modernizing visionary young ruler of Saudi Arabia and supremo of that monarchical system.

The background to this mini nation of a single family was like this. The Government of Australia had passed a Bill which led to a lot of problems for Leonard, then just a farm owner on that property of 75 sq. km. Wheat Quota Bill 1969 was passed by Western Australia Government which provided that any farmer can sell produce of his land but not more than that of ninety-nine acres. The Casley family had thousand hectares (9990) of wheat to their credit ready to harvest but the law forbade them the sale of this huge quantity except the quantity allowed under the 1969 law

Leonard tried to discuss the matter with the Government but it was to no avail. So, he finally thought of making a country of his own so that his land didn't follow Australian government diktat, particularly on the wheat Quota Bill. The Bill had two things: no compensation, no appeal. So, if any farmer had any problem with this Bill they could not demand relief nor make an appeal. So, Leonard read international laws and thought about how he could make his land a separate entity.

Eventually the country was made in 1970 to escape a law considered by one man to be unjust. Named as 'Principality of Hutt River,' Leonard declared himself as the Prince Leonard and the country became a hereditary Monarchy starting with him. Australia, formerly ruled by the British, continues to be a Dominion. The reigning monarch of the UK is also the monarch of Australia. Being in part of the Australian territory, Leonard didn't want to hurt the sentiments of the Queen. So, he didn't declare himself the king of that country, rather chose to settle with the title of 'Prince.' Perhaps on a strategic move, he invited the Queen of England to be the Head of his country to which of course the Queen politely declined. However, the country formation was done on the birth date of the Queen i.e., 21 April (Queen Elizabeth was born on this date in 1926). The Queen is said to have written letters to the Prince (Leonard) on anniversaries. Queen had a good relationship with the Prince. Prince had a problem with the Australian Government not with the Queen.

In February 2017, at the age of ninety-one and after ruling for 45 years, Casley abdicated the throne in favour of his youngest son, Prince Graeme. Prince Leonard died two years after this abdication on 13 February 2019 at the ripe age of ninety-three. After his demise, his son Prince Graeme continued his legacy as the de-facto ruler of the Principality. Their family had given up the citizenship of Australia as they lived in a separate state – the Principality of Hutt River- according to their claim. They didn't have an Australian passport.

Leonard's son says many people in the past 50 years had asked his dad if they could start their own country to which Leonard had said 'No'. You really have to know the laws and rules or else you can land up in jail. This was a unique and special case. A country by one man and one family, not on the basis of force, but on the basis of Law!

The country had its own flag, its own currency, its own passport, and its own stamp and own visa. A country is recognized as a country when other countries recognize it. Australia said this country was only made to save taxes. They only had a letter from Queen Elizabeth where the Queen had congratulated the Prince on the anniversary. The family of Leonard only stays there and did not enjoy the benefits the Australian citizens get. It is compulsory for all Australian citizens to vote. These people did not vote in Australian elections.

The principality as pointed out was not officially recognized by the Australian government, or by any other country. But it acted like an independent nation. Its government granted visas and driver's licenses, issued passports and currency, produced its own stamps, flew its own flag and reportedly operated thirteen foreign offices in ten different countries, including the US and France.

Leonard had justified his declaration of independence and secession from Australia on the basis of his personal interpretation of, what is said to be some obscure English common laws (part of the basis of Australian law) and international laws that he strongly believed allowed him to form what he termed an independent "Self-Preservation Government." Soon thereafter, he styled himself 'His Royal Highness Prince Leonard I of Hutt' and handing out regal titles to his family and supporters (who would hardly number 30), while defiantly continuing to sell wheat across their newly founded state's international border.

Revenue to this mini state was earned from fees on Visa stamping and sale of Souvenirs (normally priced at 10 Dollar each).

At the time of his ascendance, Leonard's most ambitious plan was to establish a permanent community of citizens within the limits of the 'nation'. His long-range plan was to get some sort of letter of understanding from the Australian Government so the Principality could exist without interruptions and control by the Australian government. But it did not happen. Pandemic Covid19 brought about many unanticipated changes all over the world. It played spoilsport with the micro nation – Principality of Hutt River-too. Its tourism revenue stopped all of a sudden. In December 2019, the principality announced that it would close its borders and cease its external government services as of 31 January 2020, until further notice. On 3 August 2020, the Principality was formally dissolved. But its website (http://www.principality-hutt-river.com/) remains, though nonfunctional, as a memoir of History. The Principality is said to have surrendered to Australia and the property was notified to be on sale. Though the Principality is gone, the History continues and it would certainly continue attracting more and more tourists in times to come once the normalcy is restored. Prince Graeme hoped the story of Australia's oldest micronation would be remembered. "That's the history, and you can't unwrite it," he had said. One of its officials wrote: While PHR is gone it will not be forgotten." At the end, it may not be out of place to say that the Principality of Hutt River was never able to convince an Australian court that it did not have to pay tax. As Justice Rene Le Miere of the WA Supreme Court noted in 2017, "Anyone can declare themselves a sovereign in their own home but they cannot ignore the laws of Australia or not pay tax."

Principality of Hutt River was comparable in size to Hong Kong, though it is larger in physical size than many countries such as Vatican, San Marino, Monaco, and Nauru to name but a few.

Umuganda as Patriotic Agenda with Cow as the Key to Discord and Accord

Imagine a country whose GDP growth rate had fallen to -50 percent. A country in which 15% of the population died in a horrifying genocide. 25 years later, the same country becomes so neat and clean that it is now called the Singapore of Africa!

The African state of Rwanda had the horrific ethnic strife in which an estimated twenty thousand people perished in four days of fighting. Within a span of one hundred days at least eight hundred thousand people were killed. It is a small country in Central Africa, known as land of a thousand hills because there are lot of small hills that dot the country. The country is a landlocked one with Uganda in the North, Tanzania to the East, Burundi in the south and Congo in the West.

Historically, it is said, eighteen clans were there in Rwanda which is like tribes. Each tribe had its way of socio-economic organization and categorization. People were divided basically into two communities -Tutsi and

Hutu, like India's caste system – high and low. Thus, with time it became principally two ethnic groups. Rwanda was colonized first by Germany and then later by Belgium.

Like the British who played Divide and Rule policy in India, similarly when colonizers came to Rwanda the difference between Hutu and Tutsi people were built up and the divisions accentuated so that they began to consider themselves as different Races. This happened when Belgium issued Racial Identity cards in 1932. They defined strict criteria for who will be Hutu and who will be Tutsi, especially using their physical feature as the basis of differentiation. Like people with a certain shape of nose would be a Hutu, and with certain shape of face would be a Tutsi. In fact, they also said people with more than ten cows would be Tutsi, and those with less than 10 cows would be Hutu. After this racial categorization it was found 15 percent were Tutsi and 85 percent were Hutu. The Tutsi community was considered to be the elite of that country, a ruling community, because the monarch had hailed from that community before colonial takeover. As per classification, those who had more than ten cows would be Tutsi, and then Tutsis would be considered a rich class.

When Rwanda got freedom in 1962 there was lot of hatred between the communities. Some Rwandan politicians helped in making the situation go from bad to worse. They spread a lot of hatred between the two by saying many bad things as "The Hutu and the Tutsi communities are two nations in a single state". Though they shared the same physical space, they were as if the inhabitants of different zones on the planets. Hatred between these two communities were growing but it escalated slowly step by step. There would be outbreaks of ethnically motivated violence that would send hundreds of thousands of Tutsi refugees into neigbouring countries. Children were separated in school. The Tutsi and Hutu would sit in segregated areas. If a student could not answer a teacher in the class about the community to which the student belonged, he or she was asked to get it from the home the next day. Militia groups were formed claiming they were advocating Hutuness. Basically, civilians picked up gun saying they were proud Hutus. That they wanted to establish a Hutu country, calling Hutu a way of life.

Talking about Hutuness, Media poured oil to the simmering fire. The Radio Rwanda spread hatred. Many pamphlets were printed and distributed saying any Hutu who is married to Tutsi should break their marriage and do away with such wives. Hutu should not do business with Tutsi. On 6th April, 1994 things reached the tipping point. Their president Juvenal Habyarimana, a Hutu was on aeroplane and the aeroplane was shot down. And all the people in the plane got killed including the President. Till today, it is not known clearly who exactly shot down the plane. But Hutu extremists blamed RPF (Rwanda Patriotic Front), a Tutsi rebel group. On the contrary RPF blamed Hutu extremists saying they knowingly shot the plane because they were looking for an excuse to start genocide. Whoever the culprit might be but this was a tipping point for what followed as Rwandan Genocide. In the next one hundred days eight hundred thousand people were killed by Hutu extremists. Most of the people killed were Tutsi. But moderate Hutu were also killed. The population of Rwanda was seven million and almost one million were killed in this genocide. This is the time when GDP growth rate fell to -50 percent.

The hundred days of 1994 was a dark chapter in Human History, a second of its kind in modus operandi after the Nazi holocaust. The UN and the International Community had failed the hapless people of Rwanda in protecting them. UN Peace keepers who were present at that time withdrew the next day after some ten Belgian peacekeepers were killed. The US which had lost soldiers in peace keeping in Somalia a year before was not committing its soldiers for peace in Rwanda. Soon afterward, the radio stations in Rwanda were broadcasting appeals to the Hutu majority to kill all "Cockroaches and Snakes," meaning Tutsis in the country. It was aided and abetted by the army and the national police who directed the slaughter, sometimes threatening and killing moderate Hutu civilians too. Tutsis were identified on the basis of their Identity cards. Hutu husbands killed their Tutsi wives as they were called upon to do so. So also, the Hutu neighbours would exterminate the Tustsi neighbours. Thousands of innocent people were hacked to death with machetes by their neighbors. Radio read out the names and people were picked up from homes or places of shelter like Churches or Schools to be killed in cold blood. Some prayed to be killed in a soft way. President Bill Clinton had later called America's failure to do anything to stop the genocide "the biggest regret" of his administration.

But the next 20 years is about the rebounding of their nation. The genocide ended when the Tutsi dominated rebel group RPF recaptured Kigali, the capital city The existing Hutu government got overthrown. And they seized power. A new constitution of the country was drafted guaranteeing equal rights for all Rwandans. A transitional government was formed where president who is Hutu and Vice President Tutsi. Later in April 2000, Paul Kagame became the president of Rwanda. And still, he is the President of Rwanda. Over the next 20 years amazing growth can be seen in Rwanda. On an average 7% GDP growth rate every year for 20 years. Their GDP per capita also increased to almost four times. If you compare 2000 and 2020 you see a sea change.

Apart from this they specifically focus on the education and health care section where they allocate 15 percent of budget for education and 8 percent for health care. Because of this literacy growth rate took a huge leap. In 1978 there was 38 percent, now it is around 75% literacy. The average life expectancy was 55 years in 2005, it has crossed to 69 in 2020. The ease of doing business has improved, with Rwanda now ranking 29th worldwide. This makes Rwanda the only low-income country in the top 30. They claim it is easy to register and authorize a business here and it takes only 24 hours. In 2017, Rwanda was ranked as the third least corrupt country in Africa according to the Corruption Perceptions Index. Things have improved so much that it is known as Singapore of Africa. The Rwanda government is also very open to new technologies. In 2020, the government had allocated a dedicated budget for blockchain project. Their minister had said blockchain will be instrumental in fourth industrial revolution. In 2020 the first Blockchain Training School was established in Rwanda to educate and train people about blockchain – one of the new technologies that uses robotics and artificial intelligence. The school is critical for training professionals, entrepreneurs and policymakers.

Still, it is a poor country. Approximately 90 percent of the population is employed in agricultural sector and farming. The poverty rate is worse than in India. Rwanda is 38 percent while India is less than 30 percent. Their GDP per capita is less than half of India's GDP per capita. The significant thing about Rwanda is that there is lot of cleanliness. Plastic bags are banned in Rwanda from 2008. There are different dustbins for different kind of waste and abundant in their country. They have automatic pipe system to water their flowers trees in the main road. They have another secret to maintain cleanliness callled Umuganda. Umuganda's real meaning is "coming together to achieve a common purpose." It is a mandatory community service. Their president used this strategy to make the country clean. On the last Saturday of every month from 8 to 11 in the morning, all citizens would come out and help in cleaning the country. And it would be compulsory for each citizen to participate as long as they are of able body and between 18 to 65 years of age. Penalty is imposed on them who don't participate. It is like patriotic agenda for them now. Every month even President, ministers and politicians also do their part of Umuganda. As a result, it is now acknowledged that the city is one of the world's tidiest major capitals. As a CNN report says, "Driving through Kigali, the cleanliness and the lack of trash has to be seen to be believed. There is not a speck of refuse, not a piece of paper, not a thrown away plastic bottle."

But more than the Cleanliness, it is the Brotherliness. Umuganda is seen as part of a wider healing process going on across Rwanda. The government has also restored the tradition of Girinka, a welfare scheme in which vulnerable families are given their own cow. Meaning "may you have a cow," Girinka has played a huge role in bringing society back together.

Cows are held in high regard in Rwanda. It is an assurance against the toughest forms of economic insecurity. And when a cow has a calf, it's expected that its owners will give the newborn to their neighbor. The idea is to foster community through traditional means.

"If you want to wish someone wealth, you give him a cow," says Edouard Bamporiki, a poet, an actor and Rwanda's cultural minister. And to quote him, "…if I give a cow to you, it's like we're sealing our friendship. You can't betray someone who gives you a cow."

Interestingly, during his 2018 visit to Rwanda, Indian Prime Minister Mr. Modi gifted 200 cows to poor villagers who did not own a cow in Rweru Model Village, in the presence of Rwandan President Mr. Paul Kagame.

PM Modi gifted 200 cows to a village in Rwanda in 2018 .The cows were presented to show India's support to the Rwandan presidentRwanda President Paul Kagame's Girinka programme.

A Small Country Playing A Big Role On The World Stage

The small country we are talking of is the mountainous picturesque Switzerland. It is just not beautiful, but the world's most expensive country. It is famous for many things like tourism, chocolates, watches, and above all the much talked about Swiss Banks that stack money of many politicians from different countries and the other rich. Its city Zurich is the most expensive city in the world. The cost of living index (general index) is a pointer to compare the cost of living in different cities across the world. The cost of living in the base city is always expressed as one hundred. New York City of the U.S. was taken as the baseline (whose cost of living index is one hundred) while calculating the index, the cost of living in the destination is then indexed against this number.

New York is counted as one of the most expensive cities in the world. There are only six more cities which are more expensive than New York and their cost of living is more than that of New York. Interestingly, all of the six cities are in Switzerland, they are Zurich, Lugano, Basel,

Geneva, Lausanne, Bern. The cost of living index of India is twenty-four, Zurich is 131.

The reason behind some countries being very expensive and some being less expensive or inexpensive is that there is some common pattern between developing and developed countries. A generalized theory behind this may be pointed out, five hundred years back India and China were richer in comparison to Europe. The reason, it is said that humanity at that time revolved around agriculture. It was the time of the Agricultural Revolution which along with home or cottage manufacturing provided self-sufficiency for people. But when the Industrial Revolution came, it started in Europe, after the advent of which, the economy of the world started to revolve around the industries. The theory states that the climate was very comfortable in countries like India and China and since the land was very fertile for agriculture, the people could lead their lives easily. But the climate in Europe was extremely harsh. It used to be very cold there. Necessity is the mother of invention. The climatic and environmental conditions forced people to innovate and that is why it is said that the industrial revolution began in Europe and not in India or China. And since the world economy today revolves around the Industrial Revolution, the European countries obviously forge ahead.

Switzerland is famous for its luxury watches, chocolates, and the highly developed tourism sector.

There are a lot of rich people in Switzerland. According to statistics, Switzerland has the highest per capita of millionaires that amounts to 11.8 percent of their adult population. That is, every 10th person you come across on the street of Switzerland is a millionaire. The country attracts millionaires. The reason for that is the tax here is very low. The country does not charge so much for business. The VAT rate is one of the lowest. It is around 8 percent on most of the things. It is around 7.7 percent in restaurant. It is 3.8 percent for accommodation and services, 2.5 percent on the basic necessity items. There is a huge advantage of living in an expensive country, if you are earning in the same currency. The second reason is the banks are highly safer. They have remained historically popular for the people who wanted to export their money out of their countries and indulge in money laundering. Third, it is a very safe and stable country, so obviously rich people would like to stay where there is safety and no fight.

During Hitler's rule and Nazi persecution, many millionaires of Europe crossed over to Switzerland because it was a safe and neutral country. So, when millionaires who also have been entrepreneurs come, it will have a huge boost to the country's economy. Therefore, the cost of rent, all the buying items would increase as millionaires can afford it. Not to be surprised, if so many rich people are staying in a rich country, then automatically the cost of living would increase. The richer people are in a place that is directly proportional to the cost of living of that place. So, these are the reasons why Switzerland is an expensive country.

Prosperity of a country also depends on the political atmosphere of the country. Hobbes, the English philosopher, has long since emphasized the need of political stability without which there can be no development. In a country riddled with internecine warfare, projects like science, arts manufacturing and even farming, would be impossible or a waste of time as people cannot reap the benefits of their labor, something the philosopher of strong government had cautioned. His thesis is borne out by the fact that

Switzerland has not fought any major war for last five hundred years.

As the Time magazine would tell us, the last time the Swiss fought a military battle was five hundred years ago by losing a devastating war against the French at the Battle of Marignano (September 1515). Some two hundred years ago (1815), Switzerland was acknowledged as a neutral state by the European big powers in the Vienna Congress following the Napoleonic wars. But in 1920, the League of Nations formally recognized its neutrality. Swiss neutrality is one of the main hallmarks of Switzerland's foreign policy. It dictates that Switzerland is not to be involved in armed or political conflicts between other states. This policy is self-imposed and designed to promote external security and ensure peace. Switzerland's neutrality allows the country to act as a mediator between countries at war and having enmity. Its diplomats often represent the interests of countries that have no diplomatic relations with each other. Thus, for example it looked after US interests in Cuba and Iran, and Cuba's interests in the US. It is of interest to note that its city Geneva houses around two hundred international organizations and diplomatic missions from about 170 countries. Thus, it functions as the international capital of Switzerland. It is the European headquarters of the United Nations and headquarters of the International Committee of the Red Cross.

Granting asylum to political refugees has long been a Swiss hallmark, and one of the ways Switzerland influences global politics despite its neutrality. It welcomed Russian jeweler Peter Carl Fabergé and German author Thomas Mann, along with 300,000 others during the Nazi era alone. (if TIME magazine is to be believed)

There should not be a misconception that Swiss people are not concerned about their own defense and guarding their borders. It maintains a strong army of more than 600,000 men. The Swiss Army can be mobilized in half an hour. A huge percentage of their population is ultimately military trained. During the second great war, Switzerland needed to defend its borders from both Allied and Axis air intrusions. For instance, they shot down nearly a dozen German planes in 1940 alone, as well as shot down some American bombers and forced down countless others on both sides. This included grounding and detaining the crews of over a hundred Allied bombers that tried to fly over the country.

Not to be forgotten is the fact that Switzerland is credited with being home of Direct Democracy. Here people control public policy and policy makers through instruments of Direct Democracy as Referendum, Initiative and Recall.

The Swiss generally attribute their good fortune to their national virtues like democracy, federalism, stability, neutrality and political moderation. Key to understanding of Swiss neutrality is what Churchill had highlighted as four elements that, to his mind, gave Swiss neutrality its distinctive character: Swiss Democracy, its 'armed neutrality,' humanitarian mission, and business activities.

To its discredit Switzerland was too conservative to give political equality to women for a long time. However, the blot was removed when women were enfranchised on the national level in 1971. But in the canton of Appenzell women had to wait until 1990 for full voting rights.

(Compiled from different sources).

Letters from a Father to a Son

Letters from a Father to His Daughter is widely known as letters written by Jawaharlal Nehru to his daughter Indira Nehru. These letters were sent in the summer of 1928 when Indira was 10 years old. It is said to be originally published in 1929 by Allahabad Law Journal Press at Nehru's request. It consisted of only thirty letters. A second edition was arranged by the author in 1931. Subsequently, it has gone through so many reprints and editions.

The letters are admired by many as educative pieces, seeking to explain how the world came to be as it is. At the time of the writing of the letters, Nehru was in Allahabad, while Indira was in Mussoorie. Though original letters written by Nehru were in English, these have been translated into many other languages in course of time. The famous Hindi novelist Munshi Premchand had translated it into Hindi under the name Pita Ke Patra Putri Ke Naam. In 2018 Cuba published an amplified new edition to mark the 100th anniversary of the correspondence between Jawaharlal Nehru and Indira Gandhi. In that edition, five other letters were published.

While these letters cover everything from the Big

Bang to the ancient civilizations to the rise of the division of labour and trade, we also see here a foundation of moral values for peace, justice, respect for those different from us, and immeasurable, indiscriminate kindness, as commented by some.

But the letters we are speaking of here are no less important though written in a different land, in different context and time with a different focus, by a father to his son – Mohan Das Karam Chand Gandhi to his son Manilal- which have their perennial practical value. Here we get glimpses of the Mahatma, how human he was in nature, feeling for children as other human beings have, yet so humane in approach and forward looking. These letters speak for themselves; one may say these are self-explanatory. These may sound like normative 'do's and 'don't's, but they are the alternatives—a way of thinking and living that Gandhi is known for.

Volumes have been written on the Mahatma and are still being written, He has also written volumes – in terms of letters – answering questions and queries from every nook and corner of the world. But here we talk of his own communication with his alter ego – his other son, his other self. Again, these were also many, but some excerpts are given below which are indicative of the man and his vision- his perception and perspectives. Could these become guides for our youth today? Will there be takers?

Mahatma Gandhi wrote a letter to Manilal on dated 27 September 1909 - "You got nervous at the question, 'What are you going to do?' If I were to answer on your behalf, I would say that you are going to do your duty. Your present duty is to serve your parents, to study as much as you can get the opportunity to do and to work in the fields. You need not worry about the future; your parents are doing that for you. You will take it upon yourself when they will be no more. You must be definite on this point at least that you are not going to practice law or medicine. We are poor and want to remain so. Money is required only for maintenance. He who works with his hands and feet gets his livelihood. Our mission is to elevate Phoenix; for through it we can find our soul and serve our country. Be sure that I am always thinking of you. The true occupation of man is to build his character. It is not quite necessary to learn something special for earning one's livelihood. He who does not leave the path of morality never starves, and is not afraid if such a contingency arises.

Give up all worry; do whatever study you can there. While writing this I feel like meeting and embracing you; and tears come to my eyes as I am unable to do that. Be sure that Bapu will not be cruel to you. Whatever I do, I do it because I think it to be in your interest. You will never come to grief, for you are doing service to others."

In another letter dated 24 November 1909 Mahatma Gandhi wrote: "It was good you asked the question about Phoenix. First of all, we shall have to consider how we can realize the self and how serve our country. After we do this, we can explain what Phoenix is. For realizing the self, the first essential thing is to cultivate a strong moral sense. Morality means the acquisition of virtues such as fearlessness, truth, celibacy and so on. Service is automatically rendered to the country in this process of cultivating morality.

Phoenix is of great help in this process. I believe that it is very difficult to preserve morality in cities where people live in congestion and there are many temptations. That is why the wise have recommended solitary places like Phoenix. Experience is the real school. The experience you have had in Phoenix you could not have got elsewhere.

Thoughts about realizing the self, again, could only occur to you there. The very fact that you have asked me such a profound question when you are a mere child shows your merit. The credit of your having been able to nurse Mr. West and others also goes to Phoenix. As most of the people in Phoenix are just beginners, you may find faults all round you. They may be there. Phoenix is not perfect but we wish it to become so."

In a letter dated 3 February 1914 Gandhiji had written to Manilal: "I have had two letters from you. I am also sorry I had no talk with you. No doubt, I was very much hurt that you ate chillies. It is possible that you will not feel the effects just now. But never forget that tamasic food cannot but have an evil effect. I am sure it will do you good in future if you discipline your senses.

"I can see, there has been no spiritual gain to you through your experience of jail. You have great need to cultivate thoughtfulness. It is a rare gain to have come into contact with Mr. Andrews. I should like you to take the fullest advantage of the occasion by preserving the utmost purity. So far, Mr. Andrews has expressed himself perfectly satisfied about you.

Keep an account of every pie you spend. Have no shame about doing any work for Mr. Andrews. You may even massage his calves. Having done so once myself, I know that he probably finds it agreeable. Polish his shoes and tie up the laces. You must not forget to write to me every day. Maintain a diary of meetings with all persons and the developments from day to day."

One letter dated 4 March 1914 reads: "I have your letter. You ought not to have hidden from me the fact that you lost the tin of water. Just think how much care I take even in regard to such things and take a lesson from it. But that lesson you will take only if you lay open your heart before me. You will not be able to learn anything so long as you try to hide your mistakes from me, even for a moment. Be sure that hiding or secrecy is a form of untruth, which is like poison in the system. A poison turns other healthy substances also into poison. Even a grain of arsenic is enough to render milk unfit for drinking. Insist on getting up at 4 a.m. always. If it is very cold, sit in the house, cover yourself liberally but do get up early. You may go to bed as early as you like; I do not mind that.

As regards food, you may have three meals a day if you feel the necessity. You need not control yourself in the matter of taking food. It is enough if you observe some rules regarding the articles of food. Ba is somewhat better today; but still the crisis is not over. She is bed-ridden."

In one that is dated 19 March 1914 Gandhiji says, "I hope it was after careful thought that you made the changes in diet you have done. See that whatever you do is not done in a hurry to be given up afterwards, and remembered merely as a dream. Some of it at least must endure for the whole of your life. You have introduced so big a change that you may perhaps find yourself in the same state you were in at the end of chaturmas. There is only one way to guard oneself against excessive eating, viz., to serve out the full quantity for oneself in advance and put away the utensils containing the rest before sitting down for the meal. Ba is all right."

A letter to Manilal dated 28 May 1914 reads, "I have your letter. While you express your regret, you say in the self-same letter that on that very day you had forgotten to serve so important an item as the vegetable. You say it was left out, without explaining how it happened. Who is to blame? Why did you entrust the task to anyone else?

You should have yourself carried the vegetable you had lovingly cooked. You may as well take a lesson from this. There is no need to be sorry for what is past and over, but it is important that one should learn something from it. While there, learn from its reference to the publication of the Indians' Relief Bill, which took place on Thursday, May 28. (It is clear that the letter was written the same day.)

Remain devoted to your duty and cultivate self-discipline. This cannot be achieved, however, unless one thinks. Have regard for everyone there, think of the good qualities in others, rather than their weaknesses, and be mindful of your own shortcomings. Instead of gossiping away your time, keep thinking. A single moment wasted is so much [time] lost from one's life and so much stolen from God. Understand this and use every moment well. See that your body becomes tough.

The Bill has been published and is likely to come up next week. One does not know, though. There has been no meeting yet with General Smuts."

It may not be out of place to mention that Manilal Gandhi's birth was in India, but his work place was in South Africa. Born on 28 October 1892 in Rajkot, he was the second son of Kasturba and Mohandas Gandhi. Manilal first came to South Africa in early 1897 with his other three brothers when Gandhi's family joined him in Durban.

Mahatma Gandhiji did not believe in formal education. Manilal's schooling therefore took place at home. The senior Gandhi had two Ashram's in South Africa - Phoenix Settlement (founded in 1904) and Tolstoy Farm (founded in 1910).These were important training centres and experimental schools. Manilal was one of the first experimental pupils at Phoenix.

Trained by Gandhiji, Manilal Gandhi, in 1910, then

just seventeen years old, joined the satyagraha struggle in South Africa. He fought for not only just the Indians, but all non-whites who were struggling to improve their lives and secure their rights. Between 1910 and 1913 Manilal served four prison sentences. As a champion of human rights, Manilal Gandhi is a revered name in South African history in its anti-Apartheid struggle. Former South African President Nelson Mandela had commented that Manilal's "gentle demeanour seemed the personification of non-violence."

A Towering Man on a Towering Tower

First about the Towers ! Petronas Towers are twin skyscrapers or buildings in Kuala Lumpur, Malaysia, another symbol of prestige and pride for that country. Petronas are one of the tallest buildings in the world. It was my fortune to see a little bit of Kuala Lumpur in 2017 soon after I completed my engineering and had qualified for a handful companies in on- campus selection though the academic result was still not out. Spirit was soaring so high into the sky in a holiday mood soon after I had boarded the Air Asia at Biju Patnaik International, Bhubaneswar. The Slogan of AirAsia that 'Now Everyone Can Fly' was yet to go that viral. Air Asia the leading airline established in the year 2001 was fulfilling the dream of making flying possible and achievable by everyone around any corner of the world. I was going to fulfill my dream of seeing a part of Malaysia, a country or region with which my native state Odisha (variously known as Udra, Kalinga or Utkal) had long cultural and trade ties.

From the Kuala Lumpur International Airport

down to the Downtown I was struck with its Palm dotting roads. Palm plantations line up the highways. I was truly enthralled by the first glimpse of the palms that are ubiquitous across that country. And the Skyline! Both the trees and towers were kissing the Sky in their own way, but surely complementing each other. What a development, what a country! As a child in Middle School, I had seen a bit of America about which Vivekananda had jocularly remarked, if I am not wrong, that no one should visit that country for the first time. That observation was in the closing years of the 19th Century. I had seen the Washington DC and the New York and the high rising competitions - from Transamerica Tower in Baltimore to Washington Monument in DC to still so many defiant Towers and big buildings around the ground Zero in the Big Apple with Empire Building not far off. But here I was equally awestruck with an Asian Tiger with its graceful material management. But I am no Vivekananda to say that don't visit this country for the first time.

Well, are we missing Petronas ? Yes, it is said that the Petronas, I mean the twin towers by that name, is as meaningful to Kuala Lumpur as the Eiffel Tower is to Paris and the Statue of Liberty is to New York. The iconic, soaring Petronas Towers are unquestionably the symbol of modern Malaysia. It is the heart of that nation. It is also gleefully noted that Petronas Towers have played in KL's continuing evolution into a world-class city.

Need to be stated that the name of the building came after the Petronas, the national oil company of Malaysia. Petronas were the tallest building in the world from 1998 to 2004. It was said at a point of time that it had been overtaken by a building named Taipei 101 in Taiwan. Perhaps in today's date the current tallest building is Burj Khalifa in

Dubai, UAE. Petronas is a tube structure tall building. The design of the building was done to represent the Malaysia's predominant Muslim culture. To build the Petronas tower it took almost 1.6 billion US dollars. Interestingly a bridge connects the two towers on the 41st and 42nd floors, making it the world's tallest sky bridge. There are eighty-eight stories in the building. Its length is 830 m.

Out of these two towers, Tower One is occupied by Petronas, the Malaysian Oil Major, and a number of its subsidiaries and associate companies. In Tower Two there are companies like Microsoft, IBM, etc. Indian multinational IT companies like TCS, Wipro, HCL also find place there. At the centre of the Petronas Tower is Suria KLCC. It is regarded as one of the largest shopping malls in Malaysia. There is also KLCC Park which is of seventeen acres, below the building with jogging and walking facilities. It has a fountain where light shows take place in the evening The whole scenario is really mesmerising, unspeakably beautiful and mind-blowing especially in the evening or at night.

Not very far from the twin towers, in a sort of open restaurant I could take my fond Bada, Idli and Dosa. The shop was being manned by men and women of Indian origin –the Malay Tamils. The so-called South India cuisine has become not just part of the Asian Culture, but that of world culture. These were too good, no less than the bigness or smartness of Dosas I had devoured in Indian restaurants from Birmingham to New Jersey some ten years back (2007-8). I felt myself to be in India. Kuala Lumpur has many Hindu and Buddhist temples, the famous Batu Caves being hardly fifteen kms away.

It is not about the tallness of towers, that I am going to make this presentation. It is the tallness of the spirit of a man, rather known as a Spiderman. The interesting story related to Petronas tower is that on 20th March 1997, a French climber Alain Robert tried to climb the tower from bottom to summit. He was arrested on the 60th floor, 28 floors away from the destination. In his second attempt also he was arrested, on a different tower but ironically in the same floor. Finally in his third attempt 1st September 2009, he climbed to the top in 2 hours by using only his bare hands and feet.

Robert's dangerous adventure have without surprise attracted crowds of onlookers who stop to watch him climb. The Human Spider has been arrested so many times, in various countries, by law enforcement officials. But his spirit cannot be arrested, it deserves a place in History.

Writer in front of the Petronas, KL in 2017.

Sri Aurobindo, the Great Nationalist and the Lover of Humanity

Thanks to the Ministry of Culture, Government of India, that it presented a tableau on Sri Aurobindo's life and works in the 73rd Republic Day parade that drew not only the attention of the nation on him, but that of the world. As it is now widely known, the grateful nation celebrated his 150th birth anniversary in 2022.

Sri Aurobindo does not belong to the past, but to the future, so had said Shree Maa (The Mother), his collaborator, in what one may call his Supramental Enterprise on Earth. Chittaranjan Das in Alipore Bomb case had described him in profound words that "he will be looked upon as the poet of patriotism, the prophet of nationalism and the lover of humanity." "Long after he is dead and gone, his words will be echoed and re-echoed not only in India, but across distant seas and lands," Chittaranjan had added in his pleading in prophetic words.'

"It is a fact that I was hearing constantly the voice of Vivekananda speaking to me for a fortnight in the jail in my solitary meditation and felt his presence," he wrote in his autobiography. While in the confinement in Alipore Jail, in that gloomy and solitary cell where, as he recollected in his Tales of Prison Life, he had indescribable realizations of Godhead, the Basudev (Krishna) being everywhere and in everything, it was the total and intimate identification with the Divine. As Manoj Das writes, "…in other words he woke up to his own identity, his Swarupa — that would ultimately lead him to give us a glimpse of the evolutionary future of man, the message of the Life Divine."

The Mother seeing Sri Aurobindo for the first time in 1914 wrote in her dairy, ""It matters not if there are hundreds of beings plunged on the densest ignorance. He whom we saw yesterday is on earth ;his presence is enough to prove that a day will come when darkness shall be transformed into light. "

The Prime Minister, Shri Narendra Modi while chairing the first meeting of a High Level Committee (HLC) for the commemoration on 20th December 2021 had underlined that it is the responsibility of India as a spiritual leader of the world to contribute in terms of spiritualism to nations across the globe. He suggested that 150 universities across the country should be involved in writing 150 papers on different aspects of Sri Aurobindo's life and philosophy.

The role of Sri Aurobindo, the mystic Mahayogi, in the independence movement goes almost unnoticed by today's youth. Although he withdrew from the freedom struggle, the active politics, early in prime of his career, on account of higher command, Aurobindo played a stellar role in India's march to independence. He galvanized the youth in the initial part of the struggle through his writings in "Vande Mataram." He was central to the passing of the revolutionary resolution at the Calcutta session of

Congress in 1906 which comprised universal boycott of British products, extension of the Swadeshi campaign to all of India, Swaraj and national education. It is rarely mentioned in Indian history books that the concepts of Swadeshi, Boycott and Non-cooperation were given by him long before Gandhiji appeared on India's political horizon. For his fiery writings inspiring the youth in the nationalist cause, he had been described by the Governor General Lord Minto as "the most dangerous man" in the country for the British rulers. The first-ever long debate on any Indian statesman in the House of Commons related to Sri Aurobindo.

His refuge in the French enclave Pondicherry was on a Divine mission. In reply to C. R Das who had urged him back to politics, Aurobindo had said: " Man can never get out of the futile circle, the race he is always treading, until he has raised himself on to a new foundation... The true basis of work and life is the spiritual. I am determined not to work in the external world till I have the sure and complete possession of this new power of action not to build except on a perfect foundation....I may also say that I did not leave polities because l felt I could not do anything anymore there. Such an idea was very far from me. I came away because I got a very distinct Adesh (command) in the matter."

Manoj Das, the great writer explains how two phases of his life are connected : "The first phase of his life was devoted to the liberation of the motherland. India for him was not simply a stretch of inanimate earth, but a consciousness, a living heritage of human aspiration through the ages, towards liberation of human souls from their bondage to ignorance. At Pondicherry began the second phase of his struggle for liberation — the emancipation of man from that primeval bondage."

We may do well to remember Sri Aurobindo's ideas (five dreams) in his message to the All India Radio on the eve of India's independence. The first of these was his vision of a "free and united India." But on the division of the country as it happened about, he had said, "... the old communal division into Hindus and Muslims seems now to have hardened into a permanent political division of the country. But by whatever means, in whatever way, the division must go; For without it the destiny of India might be seriously impaired and even frustrated. But that must not be."

Next, (second) India's freedom would lead to the resurgence and liberation of the peoples of Asia and India playing a great role in it. The third dream of Sri Aurobindo was " world unity" which he felt was underway. Here too India had a role to play through its right leadership and larger statesmanship. His fourth dream was the 'spiritual gift of India to the world', i.e. an increasing resort not only to her teachings, but to her psychic and spiritual practice. The fifth dream was a new step in the evolution of human consciousness (mind and man, not being the last summit in the evolutionary process) which will realize individual perfection and a perfect society. "Here too, the initiative can come from India and, although the scope must be universal, the central movement may be hers."

One thing that connects all his dreams is "Spiritualism" and centrality of India. "Spiritualism as an imperative that takes precedence over all other claims, intellectual, ethical, social that belong to the domain of ignorance....Nothing can be sufficient substitute for the spiritual change that can realize the true and integral good because through the spirit we come to the root of action and existence" the master had said. However perhaps a distinction needs to be made between Religion and Spiritualism. As the Mother said, Religions belong to the past. Spiritual teaching is above religions and strives towards a global Truth. Sri Aurobindo stands for something new and different. As one commentator has said "He was a philosopher for whom all religions were areas of enquiry. His political ideology was far more inclusive than the existing political ideologies in the world." Hope, his writings like The Life Divine, The Human Cycle, The Synthesis of Yoga, Foundations of Indian Culture and Savitri etc would show the way to the sunlit path that Sri Aurobindo has indicated. Way back in 1972, N.A. Palkhivala had commented in his radio broadcast, "It is a measure of distressing apathy of our nation that the works of Sri Aurobindo are not studied throughout the length and breadth of India. The words of wisdom from the writings of this great spirit deserve to be taught in every school and college.(AIR Bombay talk on Aug 14,1972).It is essential that India and the world awake to his writings !

A School Away from a School : My Days in an American School !

In 2007, I had an opportunity to do one year of schooling in Birmingham, Alabama, US. My father was a Fulbright Professor affiliated to the famous Miles College of that city. Under his Fulbright grant, I was eligible to travel with my mother and study free there during his two semester's tenure.

I did this schooling in Homewood Middle School. I was amazed to see the infrastructure and the ambience it had. Lovely playgrounds, a big library, and big smart classrooms, etc. It was so beautiful that I was awestruck the first time I saw it, and could not understand where I had landed.

Most schools in the USA have free education unless it is a private school. So, I had to pay no tuition fee for my studies in Homewood. Books, and other study materials and accessories were also provided to me free of cost, although after a semester we must return the books so that new students coming in can use them. Some books were hard bound and some were with thick laminated covers with prints on glossy papers. Students took care to return these in good original shape. I was amazed to know that there was no uniform of the school, I could wear any dress of my choice but it had to come under the dress code.

My first period in the day used to be sports. One hour of sports could be indoor (including gym) or outdoor. It used to be really fun and quite refreshing. I used to be very excited to go to school as I loved sports, and especially when the first period was Games. Oh yes, it was like a dream come true. We played many sports like basketball, soccer, US football. How fun it is when you are just a teen and in a new environ. A spacious sports stadium was attached to the school campus. It gave a look of a mini–Nehru Stadium of Delhi.

After the games period, I had to go to my subject classes like Maths, English, Science, History etc. There we had exams every two weeks. Their marks used to be evenly distributed, equally in all the exams save the terminal one which as I remember had a little extra. This means doing bad in one exam will not make a big impact or mar a career if someone is otherwise consistent in other examinations throughout the semester. I was recognized for my academic performance among my batch mates, maintaining an average of over 90% in most subjects, which earned me two prizes—one each semester.

I was selected for the Scholar Bowl for my good grades and performance in the class. Scholar bowl is like a quiz competition where a team of six students were chosen to represent their school. It had a concept of Home game and Away game. In Away games we used to travel to other schools to compete and in Home games different school teams came to our school to compete. I soon became the captain of my team after performing well in initial games and it was a matter of honour and achievement for me to lead an American school team being an Indian just introduced to their system. While going for an Away game, I remember we used to travel in luxurious buses, and before entering the bus we had bands and cheerleaders encouraging us to do well. It used to be a great motivation and we used to feel electrified. We used to get beautiful snacks and food in "Away Games" and "Home Games."

I had made some very good friends over there whom I met during the weekends for a soccer game or just to hang out. These were friends I could call when I was absent from school, which, of course, happened very rarely. They used to provide me with information about what was done in the class. They were super helpful.

One early morning I noticed Kevin Madox, the Principal of the School washing the plates of students after they had taken the breakfast. He at times was there at School gate supervising the traffic as parents would drop their children early morning or pick them up after the school hours. Madox tried to sow values of leadership in students. While some came by School Buses, many came by their private cars. Everyone used to be in queue and no overtaking or honking. School was always a silent zone and people never talked loudly nor there was noise of any kind. He and other teachers always put up jolly smiling faces and ever ready to sort out any problem of any pupil.

Almost every second week we were encouraged to go to the School Library or County Library, and pick up one book each to study and do a presentation before we chose another book. I vividly remember I had read Animal Farm that time. I also had read many poems there and had presented the analysis of the poems and the message the poet was trying to convey. I was highly appreciated by my Principal over my presentation on the poem "Road Not Taken" by Robert Frost. All these are like my life long treasures which I can never forget. The love of teachers and classmates there is like a "once-in-a-lifetime opportunity."

Well, I should not forget mentioning another interesting story. I had been asked to send two Indian stories to be read in the class. I chose two Birbal anecdotes. These were hilarious ones. In one Akbar asks Birbal for four fools to be discovered in his kingdom and presented in his court. Birbal finds two - one, the washerman sitting on a donkey with a load of clothes on his head, saying that how he is lessening the load on the donkey; and two – a barber, envious of Birbal advises the king to send Birbal to the other world to get information about the wellbeing of his forefathers in heaven and how Birbal slips from the pyre through a secret tunnel, built on the spot earlier. Birbal appears after a few days and reports to the king that his ancestors are doing very fine in the land of bliss except one inconvenience. Absence of a barber there has made their hair grow long and services of a barber is of urgent necessity. The barber who had originally conspired against Birbal is now chosen for the great role. The two Indian stories were so much liked that these were circulated across classes and Schools in the Homewood School chain.

Thanks to my SCB Medical Public School, Cuttack, it had given me a good grounding in English which helped me to stand up to the challenges of education in English in an American School system. Again, my familiarity with computers and their basic applications—I had learned it at home. Most of the communication between school (teachers and administration) and the student or his/her parents/guardians were on-line. The training at my Cuttack school and home stood me in good stead there in the U.S.

Thanks to the pandemic –Covid 19, the schools in India and in developing countries have exposed their students and teachers to virtual mode of teaching and learning only recently. A globalised world requires efficiency in the English language and with that the Computer Application and IT learning. My short stint in an American School as a student convinced me about the importance of English and IT for proper communication across cultures.

About a Historical Man and a Historical City

The man about whom we are talking here is another great historical figure, Ho Chi Minh and the city, named after him, is the Ho Chi Minh City (HCMC), formerly called Saigon.

Ho Chi Minh, the former President of North Vietnam was one of the most influential Communist leaders of the 20th century, though he himself had once declared that he was a 'nationalist' not a 'communist'. He led the Vietnamese nationalist movement for more than three decades, fighting first against the Japanese, then against the French colonial power and then the US-backed South Vietnamese. Ho Chi Minh was President of North Vietnam from 1954 until his death (September 2, 1969). He is also called the father of Vietnam. Original name of Ho Chi Minh was Nguyen That Than and he was born on 19 May 1890 in Hoang Tru, a place in central Vietnam. Vietnam was then a French colony, known as French Indo-China, but under the nominal rule of an emperor. Ho's father worked at the imperial court but is said to have been dismissed for criticizing the French colonial power. In 1911, Ho worked as a cook on a French steamer and travelled widely across various ports and cities. He lived in London and Paris, where he worked, in turn, as a gardener, sweeper, waiter, photo retoucher, and oven stoker. He was a founding member of the French communist party.

In 1919 Ho Chi Minh had submitted an eight-point petition to the great powers at the Versailles Peace Conference (that concluded the World War I), seeking self-determination and independence for the Vietnamese people. In the petition, Ho demanded that the French colonial power grant its subjects in Indochina the same basic freedoms and equal rights as those enjoyed by the French people.

This act of petitioning did not get a favourable response from the peacemakers, but it made him a hero overnight before many politically conscious Vietnamese. In 1923, he visited Moscow for training at Comintern, an organisation created by Lenin to promote worldwide worker's revolution. He travelled to southern China to organise a revolutionary movement among Vietnamese exiles, and in 1930 founded the Indo-Chinese Communist Party (ICP). He spent the 1930s in the Soviet Union and China. After the Japanese invasion of Indo-China in 1941, Ho returned home and founded the Viet Minh, a communist-dominated independence movement, to fight the Japanese. He adopted the name Ho Chi Minh, meaning 'Bringer of Light'. At the end of World War II, the Viet Minh announced Vietnamese independence. The French refused to give up their colony and in 1946, war broke out. After eight years of war, the French were forced to agree to peace talks in Geneva. The country was split into a communist north and non-communist south and Ho became president of North Vietnam. As a nationalist, he was determined to reunite two parts of Vietnam –North and the South. By the early 1960s, North Vietnamese-backed guerrillas, the Vietcong, were attacking the South Vietnamese government. In its designed policy of containing the spread of Communism, the United States provided increasing levels of support to South Vietnam. By 1965, large numbers of American troops were arriving and the fighting escalated into a major conflict. Ho Chi Minh was in poor health from the mid-1960s and died on 2 September 1969. When the North Vietnamese forces took the South Vietnamese capital Saigon in 1975, they renamed it Ho Chi Minh City in his honour.

"All men are created equal; they are endowed by their Creator with certain unalienable Rights; among these are Life, Liberty, and the pursuit of Happiness." — the first lines of the Vietnamese Declaration of Independence, Ho Chi Minh had issued on September 2, 1945, quoting the American Declaration of Independence. Ironically, it was the American forces that the Vietnamese would be fighting after two decades, a conflict that would stretch nearly ten long years.

The Vietnam War, also called American War in Vietnam, one of the bloodiest wars in the Cold War period involved US, the Superpower from 1965 to 1975 in a poor country, in a war in the "jungle rice-paddies" of Vietnam. Yet 'a little fourth-rate power' like North Vietnam to use Henry Kissinger's words could humble the mightiest power on earth, of course at a huge cost. The human costs of the long, protracted conflict were too harsh to describe, with a toll of more than two million civilians on both sides, over one million North Vietnamese and Viet Cong fighters, and approximately 58,000 US soldiers. The U.S. military's use of horrific napalm bombs in Vietnam triggered widespread student protests in American University campuses.

It is meaningfully said that everybody should know and learn about Vietnam war. It is of interest to know that Ho Chi Minh had visited India thrice, first in 1911, then in 1946 as the head of state making New Delhi his stopover while on way to France for peace meeting. He also paid an official visit to this country in 1958 as the President of the Democratic Republic of Vietnam. Ho Chi Minh had also participated in the Bandung conference in 1955. In an interview in 1955, Ho had said that he honoured the spiritual leader of the Indian people, Mahatma Gandhi as his master while he struggled against imperialism in Asia.

Vietnam Ambassador Pham Sanh Chau on the occasion of unveiling ceremony of the Bust of Ho at the Kautilya Marg Park in Chanakyapuri, Delhi in 2021 had said, "Uncle Ho wrote over sixty articles, research papers, poems, letters, telegraph messages & speeches about India and his experience with Indian leaders. His in-depth knowledge about India and its people and his close association with the then Indian Prime Minister Jawaharlal Nehru has helped cement Vietnam-India relationship." (By the way, this was the second bust of Ho Chi Minh to be installed in India; the first one being located in Kolkata, installed in 1990) Pham while recalling support of Indians for the Vietnamese independence movement, had said, "India supported Vietnam's independence from France, opposed American involvement in the Vietnam War, and supported the unification of Vietnam."

Paying tribute to the late Vietnam National Movement campaigner, Chief Guest of the above mentioned Bust Unveiling Ceremony, India's Minister of State for External Affairs Meenakashi Lekhi had remarked, "I'm happy to be here to pay my respect to President Ho Chi Minh whose love for our country laid the foundation of Vietnam- India relations on politics, diplomacy, economics, defence-security, education-training, science and technology and people to people relations. The present political structure of both counties may be different, but we share a strong historical and cultural bond."

India and Vietnam are celebrating their 50 years of their diplomatic ties in 2022. PM Modi has described Vietnam as a pillar in India's Look East Policy and an important strategic partner in India's Indo-Pacific vision. Answering a question Indian Ambassador to Vietnam Pranay Verma, had remarked, "Diplomatic relations between India and Vietnam were established in 1972. However, our friendship and close relations predate that milestone. We have millennia old civilizational connection, which are manifest in our shared Buddhist and Cham

(One of the two tanks whose gate-crashing into the Presidential Palace that signalled the fall of Saigon in 1975)

heritage. XX The depth of our ties has been affirmed frequently in our relations, most notably when we elevated our relations to a "Comprehensive Strategic Partnership" during the visit of Prime Minister Modi to Vietnam in September 2016."

Vietnam in general and HCMC in particular have many sites of historical and cultural importance to visit. In HCMC among others the must-see attractions for outside visitors are Cu Chi Tunnel, War Remnants Museum, Notre Dame Cathedral Basilica of Saigon and the Post Office, and most significantly the Independence Palace. I had the privilege of visiting the Independence Palace (also known as Reunification Palace) in Ho Chi Minh city and standing before the two tanks whose gate-crashing into the precinct signaled the fall of Saigon in 1975 and liberation of South Vietnam, leading to its unification with the North.

About a Monument that Swears in the Name of Democracy

The monument we are speaking of here is the Democracy Monument in the Heart of Bangkok, the capital of Thailand. Bangkok is well known as the Venice of the East. In 1932 a coup d'état by a military junta (also known as the "Siamese Revolution of 1932") had led to the establishment of a constitutional monarchy in what was then the Kingdom of Siam. The coup was led by a military leader, Field Marshal Plaek Phibunsongkhram (Phibun). It was under Phibun that the Democracy monument was commissioned in 1939 to commemorate the 1932 revolution.

The Democracy Monument is situated near to the famous Khaosan Road in Wat BowonNiwet, Phra Nakhon, Bangkok. The design of this monument was done by Chitrasen Aphaiwong. The construction was closely monitored by Italian-born artist, Silpa Bhirasi. At the time of construction of this monument it was highly unpopular, and people were unexcited as the space required for the monument meant shopkeepers and residents had to be dislodged from their shops and homes respectively and many trees had to be cut there.

The monument center has a carved representation of a palm leaf manuscript holding the Thai constitution of 1932, on top of two golden offering bowls. The constitution is surrounded by four wing like structures representing four branches of Thai armed forces – army, navy, air force and police which carried out the 1932 revolution. The central tower is three meters representing the month of June (which is 3rd month according to Thai calendar). The four wings are twenty-four meters and so as the radius of the base of the monument based on 24 June when the revolution took place in the year 1932. There were seventy-five small cannons around the outer ring of the monument representing the revolution year 2475 according to Buddhist calendar. The six gate of the center tower represents the six policies of the Phibun regime: independence, internal peace, equality, freedom, economy, and education. Naga fountains are found at the base of two wing structures. Naga depicts the protective snake creatures of Hinduism and Buddhism mythology. It also resembles the western dragons. The panel in one of the towers titled "Soldiers Fighting for Democracy" shows how their army is fighting for democracy. The panel titled "Personification of the People" shows a soldier protecting the Thai people while they go about their civil pursuits. The panel titled "Personification of Balance and Good Life" represents the social ideology of the military regime. Interestingly Monarchy is the most striking feature conspicuous by its absence from the iconography of the Monument, though it is the focal point of Thai national life and political culture even today.

Thailand has seen a number of military coups time

and again. Interestingly the Democracy Monument has been the rallying point for people to gather in protests or demand for enlargement of their freedom and political participation or overall political reforms. Last year on November 14 Thai pro-democracy protestors gathered at this place with anti-government slogans in the banner and called for reforms of the monarchy. I had the opportunity to visit Bangkok in 2022 May and I visited this democracy monument where I saw large rally of people marking the Labour Day on May 1. Here in the rally different groups of labour committee workers were parading with Thailand flags and their group committee flags displaying vernacular slogans. Different groups were distinguished by the color of their clothing and carried different flags. It was a huge rally with a lot of people but at the same time they made sure that they were in proper queue and the road passage for different vehicles was smooth.

It was a colourful long march extending miles in which children were also taking part, slogans were being raised, people were on foot and some moving in groups on vehicles, giving a picture of people's power and a feeling of festivity. One of the banners read, "We oppose globalization" Police was controlling the procession locating itself in strategic points, but the procession itself was peaceful and just slogan mongering. It reminded me of a statement that Democracy is a process and not a State.

The Story of Singapore and Lee Kuan Yew as a unique leader !

Singapore is a small city-state in South East Asia which in many ways has become extraordinarily successful to be known as Asia's dream country and the attraction of the whole world. Its unprecedented success as a nation-state is a matter of great significance especially in the context of the fact that it lacked natural resources to create such economic wonder with influence that would go far beyond its region thanks to the leadership role played by some dynamic farsighted nation-builder. And this dynamic leader and the architect of Singapore's prosperity was none other than the famous Lee Kuan Yew to whom Singapore owes a lot.

As the story goes, Singapore was founded by one Stamford Raffles in January 1819. Then it was just a nondescript small fishing village inhabited by a thousand Malay fishermen and a few Chinese farmers. The transformation of this land from a small fishing village in the early nineteenth century to a modern and prosperous city-state today is described as an incredible story of 'from rags to riches'.

Lee Kuan Yew, (born September 16, 1923) is hailed as the founding father of modern Singapore. As its first premier he laid a solid foundation with a vision for which Singapore is what it is today. A lawyer by profession he remained the Prime Minister of Singapore from 1959 to 1990. Born in Singapore during British colonial rule, which was then part of the Straits Settlements, his parents were English- educated third-generation Straits Chinese. While the family spoke English as its first language, Lee upon entering politics acquired a command of Chinese as well as Malay and Tamil. In 1965 he made a spirited speech in Malay language (Bahasa Melayu) in Malaysian Parliament and surprised the members and people there for his ease of speaking in this language, otherwise foreign to him. With interest in acquiring new languages, he had expeditiously mastered Malay after becoming the Prime Minister.

After schooling in Singapore, he had studied at the London School of Economics before earning a law degree (1949) at Fitzwilliam House, Cambridge. He also became a socialist. Although he was admitted to the English bar in 1950, he preferred to return to Singapore in 1951 to practice law but practically for political work in mind. He became popular working as a legal adviser to labour unions and won election to Singapore's legislative Assembly in 1955, while the country was still a British crown colony.

In 1950 Lee had formed an alliance with two other political newcomers—David Saul Marshall, a lawyer, and Lim Yew Hock, a trade unionist—to challenge the hold of the businessmen on the legislative council. Lee, however, soon broke with his two colleagues to take a more radical stand, becoming secretary-general of his own party, the People's Action Party (PAP).

In 1958 in London, Lee helped negotiate the status of a self-governing state within the Commonwealth for Singapore. Elections were held under Singapore's new constitution in May 1959, and Lee campaigned on an anti-colonialist and anti-Communist platform calling for social reforms and eventual union with Malaya. Lee's party won a decisive victory, getting forty-three of the fifty-one seats, However Lee refused to form a government until the British freed the left-wing members of his party who had been imprisoned since 1956.

After their release, Lee was sworn in as prime minister on June 5, 1959.Introducing a five-year plan he called for slum clearance and the building of new public housing, the emancipation of women, the expansion of educational services, and industrialization. In 1963 Lee took Singapore into the newly created Federation of Malaysia. In elections held soon afterward, the PAP retained its control of Singapore's Parliament, and Lee thus continued as prime minister. In 1964, however, he made the mistake of entering his party, 75 percent of whose members were Chinese, in the Malaysian national elections. The growing tension between Chinese and Malays resulted in communal rioting in Singapore itself. In August 1965 Lee was told by his Malaysian colleagues in the federal government that Singapore must leave the federation. Although Lee passionately believed in the multiracialism that the federation represented, Singapore had to break away. It then became a sovereign state with Lee as its first prime minister.

After the separation, the fledgling nation had to become self-sufficient, and faced problems including mass unemployment, housing shortages and lack of land and natural resources such as petroleum.

Lee's principal aims were to ensure the physical survival of the new state and to retain Singapore's national identity. Surrounded by more powerful neighbours as China and Indonesia, Lee did not press for the immediate withdrawal of Commonwealth forces from Singapore. Instead, he sought to phase them out slowly and to replace them with a Singaporean force locally trained and patterned on, what was said to be the Israeli model.

More importantly, Lee recognized that Singapore needed a strong economy in order to survive as an independent country, and he launched a program to industrialize Singapore and transform it into a major exporter of finished goods. He encouraged foreign investment and secured agreements between labour unions and business management that ensured both labour peace and a rising standard of living for workers.

While improving health and social welfare sectors, Lee continually emphasized the necessity of cooperation, discipline, and austerity on the part of the average Singaporean. His administration curbed unemployment, raised the standard of living and implemented a large-scale public housing programme. The country's economic infrastructure was developed, racial tension was eliminated and an independent national defence system was created. Singapore evolved from a dying nation to first world status towards the end of the 20th century.

Lee's dominance of the country's political life was made easier when the main opposition party, the Barisan Sosialis, decided to boycott Parliament from 1966. As a result, the PAP won every seat in the chamber in the elections of 1968, 1972, 1976, and 1980, after which opposition parties managed to claim one or two seats. It is said that Lee sometimes resorted to press censorship to stifle left-wing dissent over his government's fundamental policies.

Lee brought his country an efficient administration and spectacular prosperity at the cost of a mildly authoritarian style of government that sometimes infringed on civil liberties. By the 1980s Singapore under Lee's guidance had a per capita income second in East Asia only to Japan's, and the country had become a chief financial centre of Southeast Asia. Mr. Lee also promoted the use of English as the language of business and the common tongue among the ethnic groups, while recognizing Malay, Chinese and Tamil as other official languages.

With tourists and investors in mind, Singapore sought to become a cultural and recreational hub, with a sprawling performing arts center, museums, galleries, Western and Chinese orchestras and many casinos.

The PAP also won the general elections of 1984 and 1988, and Lee remained prime minister, though the question of the succession of leadership became an issue during that decade. After satisfactorily arranging the succession, Lee resigned the office of prime minister in November 1990, but he remained the leader of the PAP until 1992. Lee's successor as Prime Minister, Goh Chok Tong, named Lee to the cabinet position of senior minister, from which Lee continued to exercise considerable political influence. Upon Goh's resignation as prime minister in 2004 (he was succeeded by Lee's son Lee Hsien Loong), Goh became senior minister. The elder Lee remained in the cabinet as "minister mentor," a position he held until 2011, when he finally stepped down from the cabinet. He held his seat in Parliament until his death in 2015 at the age of ninety-one. Lee Kuan Yew in 1969, within ten years of his tenure as prime minister, had transformed the tiny island state into one of the wealthiest and least corrupt countries in Asia. He was able to mould the nation in his image: efficient, clinical, incorrupt, innovative, forward-looking and pragmatic. It is said that even among people who knew little of Singapore, Mr. Lee was famous for his national self-improvement campaigns, which urged people to do such things as smile, speak good English and flush the toilet, but never to spit, chew gum or throw garbage off balconies.

Lee's "Singapore model" included centralized power, clean transparent government and economic liberalism. But his rule was criticized as a soft form of authoritarianism, suppressing political opposition, imposing strict limits on free speech and public assembly, and creating a climate of caution and self- censorship. The commentator Cherian George described Mr. Lee's leadership as "a unique combination of charisma and fear." Machiavelli had outlined two important prerequisites for good leadership – love of people for the ruler and fear of him, the latter overriding the former in a competition, but otherwise both need to be there. Lee fulfilled that – a combination of the two.

On his passing away, his son the then Prime Minister Lee Hsien Loong had paid tribute to him saying, "He fought for our independence, built a nation where there was none, and made us proud to be Singaporeans. We won't see another man like him". US President Barack Obama had described him as a giant of history, the Chinese foreign ministry calling him a uniquely influential statesman in Asia. Described as a truly transformational leader in a positive sense, Lee led Singapore from its post-colonial backwater to post-modern first-world city-state status with a hundred-fold increase in per capita income. No one would deny that Lee deserves to be credited with this honour of transformation. His foreign policy was a great success in that he relentlessly pursued strategic relationships for the benefit of Singapore. Skilfully navigating third-party disputes and avoiding taking sides, he saw Singapore establish cordial relations with the United States and Iran, Israel and the Arab world, India and Pakistan, China, Taiwan, and Japan; Russia and the European Union, as well as the biggest network of free trade agreements of any country.

True to his pledge after the split in 1965 from Malaysia, he built a meritocratic, multi-racial nation and created a highly educated work force fluent in English. Lee Kuan is credited with a three language formula for students, (mandating in 1966, the year after Singapore gained independence from Malaysia), a "mother tongue" – a language associated with their ethnicity, "English" as the main language of instruction, plus one of the three official languages: Mandarin, Malay, or Tamil. The policy he believed to be a tool not only for stronger social and national ties among a diverse population, but for better economic cohesion with China and the West. Lee had created the Prime Minister's Book Prize to encourage students who did well in both English and their mother tongue. Lee had however admitted his failings for a cause in the following words: "I'm not saying that everything I did was right, but everything I did was for an honourable purpose," he said. "I had to do some nasty things, locking fellows up without trial."

A small country, but Singapore is a big idea to be emulated by others. And Lee was a titan as a leader whose leadership styles, conviction, vision and implementation will be studied by scholars and leaders for long time to come. The rule of law, the respect for order, the belief in meritocracy, inter-ethnic and inter- religious harmony, well-functioning institutions and an incorruptible administration, were the most valuable legacies left by Mr Lee Kuan Yew.

(Facts compiled from different sources).

(Author in Singapore)

Some Glimpses from the Quit India Movement : Daring Women & Children who lived or died with or for the Flag

On August 8, 1942, the All India Congress Committee (AICC)—the central decision-making assembly of the INC— at a session in Bombay unanimously passed a resolution calling the British to Quit India forthwith. It was a demand for complete independence from British Raj. It approved "the launching of mass struggle on non-violent lines on a wider possible scale under the leadership of Gandhi ". It is said that the Quit India Movement that followed this resolution was the most significant challenge to the British rule since the Great Rebellion of 1857.

In a stirring speech at Gowalia Tank, Bombay, Gandhi told his supporters "There is a mantra, a short one, that I give you. You imprint it on your heart and let every breath of yours give an expression to it. The mantra is 'do or die.'" He urged the masses to act as an independent nation, and to follow nonviolent civil disobedience.

It was agreed and ordered by the Congress Committee to carry out nonviolent campaign. But if the leader was arrested and not present to lead, the common folks would carry it forward, each and every individual as a satyagrahi. The movement captured the imagination of the people who were ready to make all sacrifices. "Every one of you should from this moment onwards, consider yourself a free man or woman and act as if you are free. We shall do or die," Gandhi had reiterated.

British Government trying to crush the rebellion arrested all big guns including Gandhi. However, the movement would gain an unprecedented momentum which would be difficult to control immediately on the part of the British. It was also the time when the British were engaged in the second world war. On hearing about news of the arrest of their leaders ,thousands of people had thronged the streets, they came out in thousands to protest.

The Queen of the Quit India Movement:

Just before the dawn of the fateful night of passing the resolution, a police official had handed over an arrest warrant to Asaf Ali, a barrister and a Gandhian fighter . Aruna Asaf Ali ,his wife and activist accompanied him to the railway station, where she accidentally met Maulana Azad. Maulana was supposed to address a mass rally at Gowalia Tank Maidan (August Kranti Maidan).in Bombay, but now under arrest. On an impulse, Aruna Asaf Ali made up her mind to stand in for Maulana Azad. However, the meeting was declared illegal and the police ordered people to vacate the ground within two minutes. Without wasting a single minute Aruna quickly climbed onto the stage and in a furry, she unfurled the Indian flag and shouted authoritatively, " Britishers, Quit India ".This marked practically the launching of the movement. The police fired upon the assembly at the session. Aruna has been dubbed the Heroine of the 1942 movement for her courage and bravery in the face of danger. In her later years she was called Grand Old Lady of the Independence movement.

She was arrested on the spot. Complete hartals were observed in various parts of India and peaceful processions were taken out across the country. The British reacted to the slogan of Quit India not only with lathi charge but also bullets and pellets. It may not be out of place to say that Aruna Asaf Ali has been later honoured with many awards and recognitions : International Lenin Peace Prize for the year 1964, the Jawaharlal Nehru Award for International Understanding in 1991, the Padma Vibhushan in her lifetime in 1992, and finally the highest civilian award, the Bharat Ratna, posthumously in 1997. In 1998, a stamp commemorating her was issued. Aruna Asaf Ali Marg in New Delhi was named in her honour. All India Minorities Front distributes the Dr Aruna Asaf Ali Sad Bhawana Award annually.

Despite the absence of direct leadership, spontaneous protests and demonstrations were held all over the country, as an expression of the desire of India's youth to achieve independence.

Gandhi Buri, a martyr of the movement:

Gandhi Buri in Bengali translates to the old lady Gandhi and it refers to Matangini Hazra, of Tamluk of the then Midnapur district of Bengal during the Gandhian era. Matangini Hazra was an ardent Gandhian, had joined the freedom struggle after being inspired by Mahatma himself. She had participated in the civil disobedience movement and was arrested for breaking the salt law. She had rendered humanitarian work in nursing small pox and leprosies patients in the villages.

Like Gandhi, the fragile body of Matangini could not deter her from taking active roles in the freedom struggle. She was also a local voice against the British misrule and atrocities. The frail woman had participated in the abolition of the Chowkidari tax- a tax enforced on villagers by the British to fund a small local group of policemen to be used as spies against the villagers.

Born in 1870 in Hogla village located under the jurisdiction of Tamluk Police station in Midnapore, Matangini Maity (Maity her original family title), could not even pursue early education due to her penury. The abject poverty compelled her to become a child bride (with a 60 year old as husband) and a mother of a young son. She returned to her village when she was 18 years old, widowed, and childless. Hazra then began building her own establishment in her paternal village and spent most of her time spinning Khadi, helping old and diseased around in the village. At that point, little did she or anybody know that how her future would pen her as an unsung women hero of freedom struggle and history would record it in golden letters.

On September 29,1942 Matangini Devi led around six thousand protesters, mostly women, to besiege the Tamluk police station. The police tried to stop the procession, citing Sec. 144 of IPC. But the defiant Hazra stepped forward, appealing to the policemen not to take recourse to firing . But in return, she was shot at arm but kept moving forward with the flag held high. The next bullet was fired, and it hit her in the forehead claiming her life. Later her body was found lying in the pool of blood, holding the flag high, unsoiled.

And the Brave Young Martyrs of 1942 on 11th

August 1942, three days after the Quit India Movement was launched, over 6,000 students marched to the gates of the erstwhile Patna Secretariat to bring down the Union Jack and hoist Indian flag. District Magistrate W G Archer, with the help of the British Military Police had tried to stop the students from reaching the Secretariat When Archer found that his force was disproportionately outnumbered, he decided to open fire. When the Bihar Military Police and the Rajputs (Indian blood was flowing in their veins) did not follow the command, Archer decided to use the loyalty of the Gurkhas against the students. The Gurkhas did not fire on the crowd directly. Their shots were measured. They wanted to kill the one carrying the flag. But the spirit of these young men was such that when one flag-bearer was gunned down, he passed the flag on to his companion. The companion too was fallen to the ground by the bullets. As one repost says, "Like flies they fell, one after the other. "By the time the gunshots stopped, seven young souls were on the ground, martyred in the name of the flag they wanted to hoist atop the Secretariat. The students were unarmed. This Gandhian mutiny, spearheaded by students no older than 16 or 17, have immortalised the protest. One paying visit to Patna can see the life-size bronze statues of these seven men, dressed in dhoti-kurtas, with the quintessential Gandhi topi, facing the Old Patna Secretariat, a symbol of the event that transpired some 80 years ago.

The seven students were later identified as: (1) Umakant Prasad Sinha (Raman Ji) – Ram Mohan Roy Seminary, Class IX, Narendrapur, Saran; (2) Ramanand Singh – Ram Mohan Roy Seminary, Class IX, Sahadat Nagar, Patna (3) Satish Prasad Jha – Patna Collegiate School,

Class X, Khadahara, Bhagalpur (4) Jagatpati Kumar – Bihar National College, Second year, Kharati, Aurangabad (5) Devipada Choudhry – Miller High English School, Class IX, Silhat, Jamalpur (6) Rajendra Singh – Patna High English School, Class X, Banwari Chak, Saran (7) Ramgovind Singh – Punpun High English School, Class IX, Dasharatha, Patna

In another notable event ,on September 20, 1942, Tileswari a twelve year girl along with a mrityu vahini — a kind of suicide squad — had marched towards the police station in Dhekiajuli to unfurl the Tricolour. Fifteen people were killed in the shooting that day . Many people do not know about the supreme sacrifice that a 12-year old girl made during the Quit India movement for the country. Today, if Tileswari would have lived, she would have been 92. September 20 is observed in the Dhekiajuli town in Sonitpur district of Assam as Martyrs' Day. Another important fact to be noted is that as many of the top leaders of Congress were behind the bars, many women filled the gap, though not openly. They took on crucial roles independently by going into hiding and organizing and leading activities from underground. They printed and organized the distribution of leaflets, collected money, and even provided safe houses to Congress leaders working from the underground. Women also organized prayer meetings and marches, and hoisted nationalist flags. Gandhi's clarion call of "Do or Die" had spread across nook and corner of the country like wild fire. There were many a martyrdoms and sacrifices in different parts. It may not be possible to recount them all. But during this Azadi Ka Amrit Mahostav, let us pay our tribute to them all, who suffered or perished in the course of the entire freedom struggle.

(Facts compiled from different sources)

Story of a Tree that Led to a Township - A Project of Human Unity

One may say that it is a tree that led to a township. Interestingly this township is different from the traditional ones. It is Auroville, a city in the lap of Nature, situated some 11 km north-west of Pondicherry and approximately 150 kms south of Chennai. Auroville is also known as the 'City of Dawn' or as the 'City of Future.' It is described as a research and experimental township that belongs to humanity as a whole.

It was a barren land before the model city came up there. It is said that a Banyan tree had sent an SOS message to The Mother of Sri Aurobindo Ashram after a nail was hammered to its trunk to hang an advertisement. The Mother sent her team next morning to the spot where Banyan tree was present and she planned that she would have the 'City of Future' near this tree or almost the tree as the centre.

In 1965, Mother had drawn the sketch of Auroville which had the basic concepts for the city. It underlined all the important activities that would be performed in different zones of the Auroville. For other things she gave an independent hand to Roger Anger, the French architect, for the city development. Mother had instructed a couple of things : city would be divided into four zones and designed for about fifty thousand people. On the basis of those parameters Roger and his team, the engineers and city planners came up with the galaxy model after lot of discussions at several stages. At the center it will have Matrimandir, "the soul for Auroville," a place for individual silent concentration. Four zones emerging out from the center: Industrial (north) Cultural (northeast), Residential (south/south-west) and International (west). Surrounding these zones will be Green belt which has farms, forest areas. The model based on the vision of the Mother would be executed under her supervision and guidance.

Foundation of Auroville was laid on February 28th, 1968 with over five thousand people present consisting of youth, and other ages people representing 124 nations.

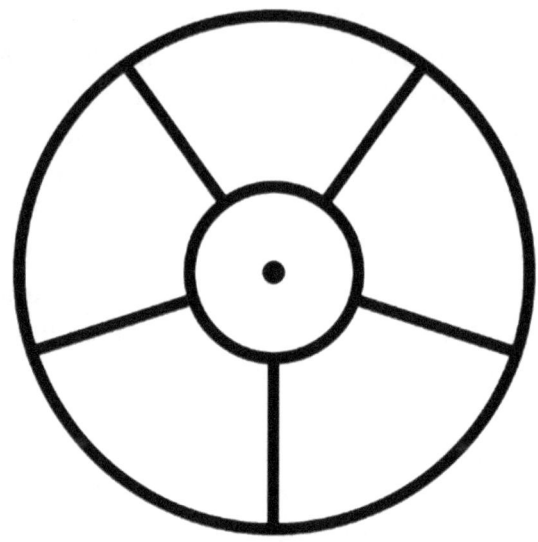

Soil from 114 countries was poured into an urn in the amphitheatre of the Auroville. The Mother read the Auroville Charter and city was unveiled. The charter has the following principles which are of great significance.:

1) Auroville belongs to nobody in particular. It belongs to humanity as a whole. But, to live in Auroville, one must be a willing servitor of the Divine Consciousness.

2) Auroville will be the place of an unending education, of constant progress, and a youth that never ages.

3) It will emerge as the bridge between past and future. Taking advantage of all discoveries from without and from within, Auroville will boldly spring towards future realisations.

4) Auroville will be a site of material and spiritual researches for a living embodiment of an actual human unity.

Auroville has a symbol. The dot at the centre of the two circle represents Unity, the Supreme; The inner circle represents the creation, the conception of the city; The petals represent the power of expression, realisation. In July 1999, the Government of India accorded special protection to the name 'Auroville' and its emblem under the Emblems and Names (Prevention of improper Use) Act 1950. The Mother has named the Hawain Hibiscus as the flower of Auroville and given it the following significance: Beauty of Supramental Love (Flower of Auroville)."It urges us to live at its height." According to the Mother a conscious and intimate relationship with flowers can give an experience of communion with the Divine and it helps awaken the true consciousness in us.

The defining symbols of Auroville include Matrimandir, the Banyan tree and urn containing the Mother's charter and handful of soils from all over the world at the time of Auroville's inauguration. The Matrimandir (also known as Soul of the City) a place for pure silence concentration is present in a large open area called Peace near to the Banyan tree. It is a large golden colour sphere which symbolizes the birth of new consciousness. The name Matrimandir means the Temple of the Mother. In Sri Aurobindo's teaching the Mother concept stands for helping the humanity to cross all its limitations and reach the next stage.

I had the opportunity to visit the Matrimandir (on Aug 16,2022). An individual who is interested to visit Matrimandir must mail the auroville authorities regarding his or her interest to visit Mandir at least 3 days before the planned visit date and according to the availability the authority will grant or deny the permission. This time I had visited Pondicherry on 150th year anniversary of Sri Aurobindo and considering the rush time, I felt completely blessed and privileged to get the permission to visit the Matrumandir and concentrate inside it.

Inside it there is inner chamber in the upper

hemisphere of the Matrimandir which is completely white, which has white marbles and white carpets. Before entering the chamber, we were given socks to wear, for the floors of the chamber to remain absolute clean. In the center of the chamber there is a pure crystal glass globe which suffuses a ray of electronically guided sunlight that falls on it through an opening at the apex of the sphere. This globe radiates natural lighting in the Inner chamber. The most important thing is the focused light of the sun in the center which is the symbol of future realisations.

We were given 20 minutes time to sit there in the inner chamber and concentrate in pin drop silence. We were told to try not to cough also, as it creates a large sound of echo inside the chamber and disturbs the quietude. In case of sneeze or cough, one is advised to go outside the chamber and complete, then come inside.

It is said that Matrimandir is there for those who want to learn to concentrate. People should sit there in silence. It is a place for trying inner consciousness. After our allotted 20 minutes we came out of the chamber and the Matrimandir and took our return Auroville bus which was provided by the authorities to reach back the Visitor Center from where we had started the journey to Matrimandir. People on a short visit, have the option to view the Matrimandir from outside, i.e., from the viewing center for which a pass is possible from visitor center.

In the visitor center one can enquire more about the Auroville and various events or activities happening in that city. There are small cafes and restaurants present near the Visitor center. Many places in the Auroville like the Visitor center, Matrimandir are headed by people from other countries, but they share the common identity of being Aurovillians. There are various workshops, therapies and other activities happening in Auroville which can be found out on their website.

To live in Auroville as permanent resident, one must be a willing servitor of the Divine Consciousness. According to the latest data in their website ninety-five people have joined in 2021. There are 3300 Permanent Residents of sixty different nationalities. Three months of volunteering before you apply, One Year – Entry process.

The International Zone (IZ), one of the four principal zones of the Auroville city that we have mentioned above hosts national and cultural pavilions from across the world, representing all the major cultures. In addition to the National Pavilions, there are also several overarching institutions in the International Zone. These are the Unity Pavilion, The Hall of Peace, Savitri Bhavan, the Auroville International Office (AVI), the Centre for International Research on Human Unity (CIRHU), the University of Human Unity (UHU), SAVI (Auroville Volunteer & Internship Service), and the Auroville Visitors Centre. The International Zone has an area of seventy-four hectares, but grouped by continents. Its central focus is to create a living demonstration of human unity in diversity through the expression of the genius and contribution of each nation to humanity.

Another place of interest in Auroville is the Cultural Zone. Planned on a 93-hectare area, situated to the east of the Peace Area, the Cultural Zone is the site for applied research in education and artistic expression. Facilities for cultural, educational, art and sports activities will be in this zone.

Forest cover in India has fast dwindled to a mere 12% due to many factors, principal reasons being industrialization and wanton felling of trees by the timber mafia. Auroville area was a lush green forest some two hundred years ago, but had become devastated in course of time. By the time the project of International Township was undertaken here, it had become completely barren from which one could see the Bay of Bengal in the East clearly without any hindrance. Thanks to the effort of the early Aurovillians, who are fondly called the pioneers, today we see a sea change – a thick lush green pleasing forest looking so natural, another identity of the City of Auroville in a green physical base, giving a lesson to others about forest regeneration, the urgent need of the hour for carbon sink and healthy living.

In Auroville one finds many skill development programs especially those which empower the locals, particularly women and children. Many voluntary groups and non-profit organizations are working primarily in the domain of Gender, Water, Sports, Business, Finance, Energy, Environment, Education, Child & Youth Development, Art & Culture and Agriculture.

It needs to be mentioned that UNESCO has adopted this unique township that is based on the Mother's vision and Sri Aurobindo's ideals. UNESCO through its many resolutions since 1966 has called upon "member states and international non-governmental organisations to participate in the development of Auroville as an international cultural township designed to bring together the values of different cultures and civilisations in a harmonious environment with integrated living standards which cater to man's physical and spiritual needs."

PM Modi in an address at Auroville in 2018 acknowledged how Auroville has been a pioneer in different fields, be it "un-ending education, environment regeneration, renewable energy, organic agriculture, appropriate building technologies, water management, or waste management." Hoping that Auroville may serve as a beacon to the world, Modiji said, "May it be the guardian which calls for breaking down narrow walls of the mind. May it continue to invite everyone to celebrate the possibilities of humanity's one-ness."

To remember again : Auroville is meant to be a universal town where men and women of all countries are able to live in peace and progressive harmony, above all creeds, all politics and all nationalities. The purpose of Auroville is to realize human unity.

Mr Nitish Nivedan Barik, at the famed Banyan Tree of Auroville

About a Friend of India, also the Friend of the Poor and Downtrodden!

'Swaraj is coming, Mohan!', he had muttered words in his death bed some seven years before it truly came. He dressed like an Indian in dhoti and kurta and would part with his woollen garments and warm clothes when he came across any poor or needy not able to fend himself or herself against a biting cold or a chilly winter. He also gave away money at the cost of going penniless many times. How he survived is a big puzzle. It was the Englishman, Charles Freer Andrews, who, as it is said, devoted half his life to the cause of India's freedom. He called Mahatma by his first name Mohan! Gandhi fondly called him, Charlie! Andrews born in 1871 in United Kingdom was a teacher, Christian missionary, priest, a social reformer and most significantly friend of India during its crucial freedom struggle days. He earned the title Dinabandhu which means friend of the poor for his love and compassion for the poverty-stricken people not only in India but all over the world. Charles had thirteen siblings and their family suffered a financial instability due to a fraud done by a friend. He underwent hardships for his finances and it is from there he developed his kindness and compassion. Andrews came to India to teach philosophy at St Stephen's college. He taught there for 10 years. He was appalled to see the injustice done by the Britishers, and therefore supported India's freedom struggle. He had connections with influential people in England and he tried to bring to their notice the undue dominance by the British officials on the Indians and their harsh sufferings.

Andrews had close connection with Gandhiji. He was asked by Gopal Krishna Gokhale to visit South Africa and help the Indian community there to solve their political disputes with Government. He first met Gandhiji (lawyer then) in Durban, South Africa who was leading the fight for the rights of Indian communities against the racism faced by them and police legislation that infringed their Civil liberties. He was seriously impressed by the Doctrine of Ahimsa (non-violence) by Gandhiji. He was an integral member of Gandhiji's ashram in Natal and helped in publication of the magazine, The Indian Opinion. He

played a major role in persuading and convincing Gandhiji to return to India in 1915.

Andrews visited Fiji, Kenya and Sri Lanka and many other British colonies to take stock of the conditions and report on the treatment of Indian labourers. He was aghast to see the conditions of indentured Indian labourers in Fiji (another British colony then). He interviewed various workers and made a report which highlighted the ill treatment of the labourers which led to the end of further transportation of Indians to British colony in 1917. The system of Indian indentured labour was formally stopped in 1920.

Andrews also had excellent bond with Rabindranath Tagore. He was part of Tagore's Visva Bharati, the experimental educational institution. A big fan of Tagore's poetry works, he translated many of Tagore's work into English. Andrews was given the task of collecting due money from parents of their children who were enrolled in Visva Bharati, but Dinabandhu being kind hearted and compassionate, it is said, he hardly pressurised them and as a result many dues remained unpaid. He often acted as an intermediary between the British administration and Indian Communities in British colonies.

He was the unifying link between Gandhiji and Tagore. In Gandhiji he saw a leader with the capability to help India gain independence from the British and in Tagore he saw creativity that could make age old conventions stand, survive and progress. It is very interesting to see how the man came initially with perhaps the agenda to spread Christianity but later felt in love and played an active role in India's struggle for freedom. He was well read and had a deep understanding of Hindu & Buddhist traditions and literature.

Andrews was elected President of the All India Trade Union Congress in 1925 and 1927. A leader against the untouchability, he also worked with BR Ambedkar for formulating the demands for Dalits in 1933.He also wrote about the atrocities against the peaceful Akali Sikh protesters by the British Police.

In 1931, he assisted Gandhi at the Second Round Table Conference in receiving him at London, setting up his office close to the Conference and putting up other logistics. During this time, he wrote letters and gave interviews to the press to highlight Gandhi. In his message to the British government, he had urged them to take the 'essentially truthful man' i.e., Gandhi (whom he knew across his 20 years in India) into confidence for right settlement of India's political issue of freedom. He wrote about Indian developments every now and then for British, American and Canadian news agencies.

Interestingly he was looked upon with suspicion by the Arya Samajists as a "missionary spy,' Also the British colonial administration equally suspected this dhoti clad and Hindi speaking Briton whose name was struck off from the list of fellowship at Punjab University in 1907. His popularity among Indians had led one member in British House of Commons demand his deportation and trial for sedition.

After his versatile role in India's struggle, he had returned to England in 1935 and came back in 1940. He was ill then and got admitted to Calcutta's hospital. He refused to receive special treatment and died like a common man. On the day of Andrew's death Gandhiji told, "I have not known a better man than CFAndrews."

Tagore also paid a tribute through a song: Love came to my life/Walking softly, silently/ Love came to my life/ I mistook him for a dream/ Didn't care to greet him. (translation of the Bengali version).

CF Andrews, a prolific writer and journalist, he wrote a number of books on India, Gandhi and Christ. The earnings from his autobiography, "What I Owe to Christ" (1932), were donated to Tagore's Santiniketan. To pay gratitude to Andews, certain institutions have been named Dinabandhu after him. Two undergraduate Colleges of University of Calcutta, the Dinabandhu Andrews College, and the Dinabandhu Institution (Shibpur Dinobundhoo Institution) and one High School in Salimpur area of south Kolkata are named after his name. In South, some hospitals have been named as Deenabandhu. One such was Deenabandhu Hospital, Thachampara, Palakkad, Kerala, later acquired by ESAF. There are two versions about his earning the title of Dinabandhu (the friend of the down trodden). One is that Gandhi bestowed it on him. But the other one would say that he earned it in Fiji for his social justice work. During the celebration of Azadi ki Amrit Mahotsav, it is worth remembering this Dinabandhu!

My MCG Moment !

It was a dream come true, my date with MCG ! I can proudly say like many other fortunate ones that I had my MCG moment.

"The MCG is one of Australia's greatest assets and sits proudly alongside other internationally recognised attractions and attracts three million-plus people annually." says one commentator.

Another sports analyst writes," Melbourne is arguably the sporting capital of the world, and that is largely thanks to one of our most recognisable icons; the Melbourne Cricket Ground."

MCG or the well- known Melbourne Cricket Ground popularly also called 'G' in Australia is the birthplace of (test) cricket. It is located in Yarra Park not far from the city centre in Melbourne, Victoria, Australia. Built in 1853, the stadium has played a profound role in the development of international cricket. MCG is the venue that has hosted the first Test (1877) as well as ODI (1971) matches that were played between Australia and England.

Teams representing Australia and England played what is regarded as the first Test match from March 15-19,

1877 at the MCG. Australia won the match by forty-five runs and the birth of international cricket is said to have taken place here then.

Interestingly the history was re-enacted hundred years after in 1977. The commemorative 1977 Centenary Test between Australia and England was again a great memorable event. With Australia struggling at 132 for four on third day of the test match and in need of a fight back, David Hookes provided one when he smoked five fours in a row. England fought back valiantly in their second innings, led by a huge 174 by Derek Randall but fell short by forty-five runs, producing the same result as the first Test 100 years before.

MCG has hosted the 1956 summer Olympics, 2006 commonwealth games and cricket world cup in 1992 and 2015. It is hosting 2022 T20 cricket world cup, currently underway as this write-up goes into print in the Literary Vibes. It is also the main venue for Australian Football league match and significantly MCG has been used for "rest and recover" by the armed forces of the US, Australia during World War II.

The first Olympics to ever be held in the Southern Hemisphere put Melbourne on the map as a stronghold of world sport, when it became the first city outside Europe and the US to host the Olympic Games in 1956. The MCG was the key venue at the Games as Australia won thirty-five medals.

Interestingly the aptly coined "Friendly Games" title was epitomised at the Closing Ceremony of Olympics at the MCG, when John Wing, a Melbourne teenager, penned a letter to the organisers of Olympics urging them that the athletes should march together rather than behind the flags of their countries separately. "There will be only one nation.

War, politics and nationalities will be forgotten. What more could anybody want if the world could be made one nation," Wing pleaded in his letter. This led to the Olympic tradition that has been followed at the closing ceremony of the world mega event since then.

It is here at MCG that Sir Don Bradman had scored his fourth consecutive century, which was repeated by Sydney great cricketer, former Australian captain Steven Smith at this same ground. Shane Warne's 700th Test wicket had happened here (December 26, 2006). It was his farewell MCG Test for the local hero Shane Warne who became the first Australian to take seven hundred Test wickets when he bowled England's Andrew Strauss enroute to a five-wicket haul on Boxing Day Test match. The crowd of about 90,000,

one of the highest crowds for a day of cricket in Australian history - went into raptures. It was the first Ashes hat-trick in 90 years. The tragic death of Warne (13 September 1969- 4 March 2022) was a shock to all cricket lovers. The State Memorial Service in his honour was held at MCG on 30 March 2022.

I had been to Melbourne this month (i.e., 3rd October 2022). I had been planning to visit this historical ground for quite some time, but a week before my trip I checked their website to book for the stadium tour. Whole October calendar was showing unavailable on the website and the reason it was displaying that the ground was getting prepared for the Mega event ICC cricket World Cup 2022. I was bit disappointed but I had in my mind to at least visit the stadium from outside. On my second day of Melbourne visit, in my itinerary I had planned Melbourne cricket ground. I reached the place; it was a pure fanboy moment for me.

Outside the stadium there were many statues in every fifty meters of Victorian Cricket legends who went on to represent country, statues of Australian football legends, Olympic athletes, etc. I felt honoured to take my picture Infront of the Sir Donald Bradman's statue. At that moment I felt it was worth coming to MCG because just taking the pictures from outside made me feel great. I could also see National Tennis Centre there. This thrilled me.

After a lot of photos, I asked a security guard present there if it was possible to go inside MCG for a tour on that date, and he said to my disbelief," Yes" and the entry for that he told me was from Gate No. 6. I was completely surprised, at the same time thrilled and felt so happy. But I was not completely convinced till I got the ticket. I ran like a child to Gate No. 6 in case it would close because it was already past 1PM. I reached there and enquired in the counter after entering the Gate and it was a dream come true moment. They told me that yes, I can book for a MCG tour, the guide will take us around the MCG Ground and show us each thing one by one. The entry fee for that is 30 AUD, I paid it gladly and I was told to wait with the other viewers who had come for a ground tour like me.

After 5 mins the guide arrived, a smart sober gentleman dressed immaculately. He introduced himself as Mr. Greig and asked all the people wating for him for the purpose of the visit. I mentioned that I'm from India, and as a huge cricket fan, I have watched numerous games played at the MCG on TV. So very excited to see the ground and other stuffs live with my naked eye. Of the other people who were there what I remember two were from Scotland who had come to see their iconic athletes home ground, and rest from Australia I believe. Mr. Greig was very friendly and he told that 'the more we can walk the more we can cover and discover more'. The tour was for around one and half hour. He first took us to the ground floor inside the stadium, I could see the dugout where cricketers' seat. I took photos there. I was near the boundary rope, but we were told we cannot enter inside the rope as the pitch and all was being prepared for the world cup. When I saw the ground, I just imagined what it would be feeling to play infront of a packed house which accommodates more than or nearly a lakh of spectators on many important occasions.

But from what I saw I felt dimensions of the ground was not huge and I could hit sixes to some part of the ground if given a chance. Then Mr. Greig told us to follow him, we then reached the Dressing room of the home Team (Victoria). Mr. Greig said, that is the place where players keep their kit bag stuffs, individual lockers and all. I had a rough idea as I am a die-hard fan but this information was new to some. In the dressing rooms there were chairs where players could sit. Then Mr. Greig took us to the next room, which was the strategy room. It had white boards, TVs and all. Mr Greig told us that this is the place where the players analyse the strength and weakness of the other rival teams. They make their strategies. After that we followed him to the press conference room, he told us that this is the place where the captain or the player who has come to addresses the press, faces the heat from the sports journalists especially if his/her side has lost.

    I was capturing all of Mr. Greig talking's in my iPhone and at the same time I was not missing any chance of taking my own photo in these special places, either by selfies or by giving my phone to someone in the group to take. Meanwhile Mr. Greig was telling hurry up, many more things to see. After getting out of the press conference room we were walking to our next spot. On the side there was indoor net practice facilities. Mr. Greig pointed out to those practice pitches and told, so our guys feel difficult to face Bumrah. So here in this indoor practice, we have a bowling machine hidden behind the screen, so players can select Bumrah and it will seem like Bumrah is running to bowl with his action and finally the ball will come out from the bowling machine through the Bumrah's hand shown in the screen. That's how they can get accustomed to his awkward action, speed and pace. But I joked him there that live games are completely different from these simulated ones which he laughed off and then we proceeded to our next spots.

    Greig took us then to the Media broadcaster rooms, where live commentary happens. Inside rooms there was already meeting going on to which Mr. Greig told them,

"Sorry folks to interrupt your discussions but these are enthusiastic visitors who want to see all these boxes." To this they happily smiled. Then we were taken into sections whose seat tickets are very expensive. Those sections outside view to the ground was covered with glasses and had AC in it. It would be comfortable watching from there. The views were great. I took photos, some photos here, and some there, everywhere. Then we were taken to a gallery where many photos of iconic moments that has happened in MCG were captured and displayed along with medals, bats and souvenirs. I could see Brad Hodge bat kept in a glass. Meanwhile I saw Great Shane Warne statue from the glass in the outside. I wanted to take a photo with that statue but couldn't figure out how to reach there as it was some distance away and difficult to reach there.

There were pictures of Olympics games held in that ground, there were pictures of their athletes. Among so many photos of greats and great actions, I could see that of Kapil Dev in bowling action, Bradman, and Tendulkar jointly in a single frame.

After such a splendid time Mr. Greig announced that we had reached from where we had started, and asked our opinion about how it was. I replied it was beautiful, life time experience and would like to take a photo with him. He happily accepted the invitation and I had a snap with him. He told me to give my feedback regarding this tour to his boss, who was a little away in his office on the same ground floor. I met his boss and told Mr. Greig had done a wonderful job, he has walked us through all the things inside the MCG, it was beautiful time, worth spending. His boss was happy and so as Mr. Greig. They asked me if I was visiting MCG again on 23rd October (that month, 2022) to see India vs Pakistan, world cup match which I told sadly

'No" as I would have left Australia by then. They told the tickets were sold out within 15 minutes of the selling and felt sorry that I was missing a great cricket festival and the most excited event as India-Pakistan duel.

I thanked both of them once again and came out of the ground happily. I have captured my tour in video and writing this article which I will always read and cherish. Definitely one will not hesitate to agree that it is a lifetime experience.

The Story of an Indian Hero on The Battlefronts in China

During Second Sino Japan War, Chinese General Zhu De, a revolutionary wrote a letter to Jawaharlal Nehru ji in the late 1930s to send some Indian doctors to treat their Chinese soldiers who were getting injured in the battle field. Netaji Subash Chandra Bose, the then President of Indian National Congress made a press statement to appeal for the same. Bose wrote an article in Modern Review on Japan's aggression on China. The key point for this mission was that India, a country then fighting for its own independence would help another country which was also fighting for the same cause. Dwarkanath Shantaram Kotnis was an Indian doctor born on 10th October 1910 in a middle-class family from Sholapur, Maharashtra. He had two brothers and five sisters. In 1938 after his graduation from Seth G.S. Medical College, University of Bombay, he was preparing for his post-graduation. At this time, he heard about the challenging opportunity to serve in China and immediately wanted to take up this job before going for higher education. Little he or his family knew about

China then. His father encouraged young Kotnis to venture out but his mother was sad and worried that he would be going to an unknown territory and serving in a war zone.

He was part of the five member doctors' team who arrived in China to help the army who were fighting on the front line. Kotnis also had to be in the front line to treat those soldiers. Needless to point out that it was a great risky venture. At one day around eight hundred soldiers were getting injured and had to be treated. It is said that sometimes Dr Kotnis had to perform 72 hours surgical operations at a stretch without sleep. It was a very stressful job, still the soldiers got the best service possible and very good treatment and recovered under Kortnis. Even while the war was not over and the missions of some foreign doctors were perhaps achieved as the locals had been trained in Medicare, and they decided to go back to their native country including Kotnis's other Indian compatriots,

Kotnis stayed back and then joined the Eight Route army in 1939 to nurse and treat. He did an effortless job. People used to come to thank him for stupendous contribution. His hard work and dedication for the country was noticed and he was made the Director of the Bethune International Peace Hospital. Kotnis swore an oath by the tomb of Dr Bethune (tomb of Dr Bethune was after the Doctor Norman Bethune, a Canadian doctor who had also been a great medical helping hand for the Chinese) that I will live the life as yours and he truly lived up to the expectation. He was very fluent in Mandarin and taught medical students at a time where there were no text books in that language. Kotnis was writing his own text books and it is said that when he was writing the second text book on page number 173, he collapsed. Later he died.

He was very happy in China and wrote letters to his family which sounded that he was happy and content with the profession he was living. Every place he went in China he would describe in detail in his letters to his family. He loved Chinese culture and the place so much that he learnt the language and became proficient in writing and speaking. His Chinese name was Kedhihua dai fu. He got lot of love from the people in China and gained popularity and was adored as a hero. That was the primary reason why he did not leave China during Sino Japan war (1937-45) described as the War of Resistance by the Chinese. He fell in love with a Chinese nurse, Guo Qinglan, in 1941 and they both married. The next year they were blessed with a son. The Child was named Yin Hua, Yin meaning India and Hua meaning China. But due to too much hectic work and pressure which Kotnis had to undergo while treating patients during the demanding time of war, he in the year 1942 died at a very young age of thirty-two due to epilepsy attack. He was buried in heroes courtyard in Nanquan village, China. His son followed his father path to become a graduate from a medical college but he also died for not getting proper treatment in 1968.

When Kotnis died Mao Zedong had said, "Army lost a helping hand and Country lost a friend, let us bear in mind his internationalist spirit." Till today also he is a sign of Sino-Indian friendship. His wife was honoured at several India China diplomatic functions which were attended by Vajpayee and before that KR Narayan. Qinglan his wife often visited her in-laws in Mumbai and passed away in 2012. Chinese delegates and officials used to visit Manorama, who was Kortnis's sister. Together they would reminisce the Doctor's great work.

School Shijiazhuang Ke Dihua was founded in 1992 and named after Kotnis. More than fifty thousand people have graduated from that school since its inception. All the new students and staff must swear before the statue that they would work like him according to Liu Wenzhu, an official of that school. Liu hopes that Kotnis is not only remembered as an icon who had served people and wounded soldiers in a hard and trying circumstances very efficiently but also as a symbol of friendship between India and China.

Madame Sun-Yat said that regarding Kotnis's role in the revolution "his memory will belong not only to Chinese or Indians but to the noble rollcall of fighters for the freedom and progress of all mankind, the future will honour him more than the present because he struggled for the future generation ". A memorial at his birthplace, Solapur was installed on 1 January 2012, built by the Solapur Municipal Corporation. The south side of the Marty's memorial in Shijiazhuang city of the Northern Chinese Province is dedicated to Kotnis. There is a statue in his honour. A small museum is there which has a handful of books written by Kotnis on his passage from India to China.

Kotnis is revered in China with their textbooks telling the story of the doctor to their children. It is said that Beijing hospital has created a medical team in his memory. "Yet his adventure and medical philanthropy is little known in the land of his birth. 'Few in Mumbai or the rest of the country know about the doctor who served in China during the 1938 Sino-Japanese war and died there in 1942,"Kotnis's younger sister Vatsala had once remarked.

But it is worthwhile to mention that the well-known film-journalist, Khwaja Abbas Ahmed had written about Kotnis in his bestseller, "One Who Never Returned" in 1945. The following year there was the screening of the classic Bollywood movie "Dr. Kotnis Ki Amar Kahani," directed by V. Shantaram.

In 2003 at a reception party in Beijing in his honour, while introducing Guo Kotnis, wife of Dr Kotnis, the then Prime Minister Vajpayee had said to the audience, "Even if you don' t know who Dr Kotnis was, you must have seen the film Dr Kotnis Ki Amar Kahani."

About Some Black Swan Events!

Black Swan event is an unexpected incident which doesn't have any previous patterns and cannot be predicted as it is too rare and are in the category of exceptions. Such events affect almost everything globally, the economy, the mankind, the living style of the people etc. Some people see this turmoil as an opportunity and rise while some organizations or individuals get trapped and never recover from this. Risk Management becomes a big challenge which needs to be planned and handled efficiently during such trying moments by the Government or the concerned authorities so that its negative impact is as minimal as possible.

Black Swan event is a phrase which was first coined by the Professor of Finance, Nassim Nicholas Taleb of New York University in his book "Fooled by Randomness" in 2001. He later elaborated the phrase through his book, "The Black Swan: The impact of the Highly Improbable" in 2007. People around the world believed and had taken it for granted that the swans were white in colour only. But surprisingly and unexpectedly in the year 1697 a Dutch explorer, Willem de Vlamingh discovered the black swans or the swans which were uni-colour black. Taking cue from this 17th century Black swan discovery the Finance professor Taleb, also an ex-Wall Street trader, tried to describe how some unexpected thing can happen which will produce earth shaking repercussions with both good or bad consequences. But people need to anticipate and make plans to deal with such most unexpected eventualities.

The Covid 19 is considered as one such black swan event as no one had predicted this phenomenon to happen as when it did in Wuhan in China and spread so rapidly throughout the world bringing life to a standstill, besides taking an unprecedented toll of life almost everywhere. In the financial world it showed the downfall of many businesses globally. On a positive side it brought fortune to some who took decisions based on long term sustainability. One such case is about the company OfBusiness start-up which became a unicorn , which as we know is a company that has reached a valuation of one billion dollars. Its CEO and co-founder Ashish Mohapatra a man from Odisha

and a product of my School, SCB Medical Public School, Cuttack and an IITian (Kharagpur), says "Everything that is tough has an opportunity. If you believe that you can make a lot of progress through it ". He said by the mid of January 2020 it was clear to all that a black swan event was going to hit the world. Most of the Chinese provinces had declared emergency in mid of January of that year but most people throughout the world went about their normal way and reacted late. You got to have leading indicators not lagging indicators and you have to react first. Global trade corridors stopped, many businesses of India which relied on China and South East Asian countries like Myanmar, Vietnam, Cambodia for imports from those countries were stopped because of which commerce became local in nature. There was no way things could be imported from outside as you don't know when things will reach you. So, globalization became localization. But Indian players stood up. During this harrowing period, Consumerization came back to India by Indian companies. Those Indian companies which were providing high quality services became bigger. Mohaapatra says businesses which lost in that covid period was because they lost trust in their people. Many Business houses started firing employees, cutting and deferring wages.

In the month of April 2020,OfBusiness, a start-up till then, which hadn't become unicorn had no revenue for that month. Still, they decided that they won't cut people cost, they won't fire any employee because once people are fired that will create chaos, panic in the organization. Employees will lose their trust on the organization. People are investment not expenses. Due to this ideal and strong conviction and integrity of the company it rose from a start up to a unicorn business.

Nicholas Taleb has described that Risk Management for investors can be handled in two ways for any kind of black swan event. One is the barbell strategy where investment should be made in safest financial products and small investments for speculative investments. No investment should be in the moderate risk and the risk bearing part of the portfolio must not be more than 10%. Maintaining a diverse portfolio is important as that will ensure if one of the investments is not doing well, the loss can be covered by other investments which are doing well. And if we correlate with Ofbuisness strategy it was similar to Taleb Risk Management. Ofbusiness bosses followed the barbell strategy in way that their safest investment is people who work for them. They didn't cut people cost, rather told them that their salaries will be increased in June. This in a way assured the employees about their salary and brought the best out of them in job. They cut costs on non-essential features, such as gathering expenses and business travel, which, like Taleb described, weren't risk factors during the turmoil.

Another such black swan incident was the black swan event of the 2008 stock market crash in the US, collapsing the whole of the Wall Street and bankruptcy of the Lehman Bros bank. Eventually US responded to the crisis by passing the American Recovery and Reinvestment Act of 2009, which was used as an expansionary monetary policy, facilitated bank bailouts and worked towards economic growth.

September 11, the cataclysmic event of terrorist attack on the twin towers of New York may be called another Black Swan Moment as it is said to have changed American society and the world as never before. It will not take hard labour to find out other Blackswan moments in history. January30,

1948 is another date when Mahatma, the apostle of peace fell to the bullets of an assassin, uttering Hey Ram, still with a calm and composed countenance , without betraying any bitterness. People remembered and drew a parallel with Christ who during those painful processes of crucification prayed God to forgive those ignorant persons as they did not know what they were doing. These tragedies or Blackswan events had their positive sides too in spreading the messages of peace and alternative approaches to issues of conflicts in politics.

About the Man Born with Large Head and Big Ears

The child was born with a large head and big ears. Rabindranath Tagore who intently looked at the facial features and shape of the head and expression of the child quietly told the parents that he would become a celebrity. That came true. APJ Abdul Kalam is known as the Missile Man of India. But Dr Vikram Sarabhai, (who Rabindranath had predicted to be a celebrity) rocketed high in achievements and reputation in a short span of time. We may call him the first Rocket Man of India. Born to a wealthy industrialist family involved in the freedom struggle at Ahmedabad, Gujarat in 1919, Vikram Sarabhai became a top scientist, physicist and innovator who also came to be known as father of Indian Space Programme.

The story of the Indian space programme, as it has rightly been said, is closely entwined with the story of Vikram Ambalal Sarabhai. He played a major role in establishment of Indian Space Research Organization (ISRO). His networking with NASA helped the creation of

Satellite Instructional T.V. Experiment (SITE) in 1975 which brought cable television to India, though Vikram was not alive to see it. He was also one of the founders of IIM, Ahmedabad. Most significantly he mentored none other than APJ Abdul Kalam, who became the 11th President of India after an illustrious career in Aerospace science.

Mr Sarabhai earned his doctorate from Cambridge University. There he studied natural sciences and published many research papers. Later he joined the Indian Institute of Science, Bangalore and worked under the supervision of the great Nobel laurate C.V. Raman. He founded the Physics Research Laboratory only at the age of twenty-eight in Ahmedabad. Russia's Sputnik satellite launch made Mr Sarabhai feel the need of a Space Agency in India. He approached the Indian government to start a body for space Research with the following note: "There are some who question the relevance of space activities in a developing nation. To us, there is no ambiguity of purpose. We do not have the fantasy of competing with the economically advanced nations in the exploration of the moon or the planets or manned space flight. But we are convinced that if we are to play a meaningful role nationally, and in the community of nations, we must be second to none in the application of advanced technologies to the real problems of man and society." His ambition, efforts and dedication led to the establishment of INCOSPAR (Indian National Committee for Space Research).It was later named as ISRO.

Vikram Sarabhai teamed up with Homi Bhabha to set up India's first rocket launching station at Thumba, near Thiruvananthapuram in Kerala on the coast of the Arabian Sea. This site was chosen primarily because of its proximity to the equator. India launched its inaugural flight to space on November 21, 1963.The flight was a sodium vapour payload. After Bhabha's sudden demise, Dr. Sarabhai took over as the chairman of the Atomic Energy Commission. He then started a project for the fabrication and launch of an Indian satellite. As a result, the first Indian satellite, Aryabhata, could be put into orbit in 1975 of course from a Russian Cosmodrome.

Beyond rocket science and technology, Vikram was also a lover and patron of art and culture. He had married Mrinalini, a classical dancer and choreographer. They both started Darpana Academy of Performing Arts in their native place of Ahmedabad. Their daughter, Mallika, is an actor and activist. Her performance of "Sita's Daughters" has been performed over 650 times in multiple countries. The show addresses issues like sex-selective abortions, police treatment of abused women, and rape testimonies

Vikram Sarabhai passed away on December 30,1971, at a very young age of 52. He died in the hotel room in Kerala after witnessing the firing of a Russian rocket and the inauguration of the Thumba Railways station. Indian Postal department released a commemorative postal stamp on his first death anniversary (30 December 1972). A crater on the moon was named in his honour in 1973 by the International Astronomical Union in Sydney, Australia.

Dr Sarabhai had been honoured with the Shanti Swaroop Bhatnagar Award for Physics in 1962 and Padma Bhushan in 1966. He was awarded Padma Vibhushan posthumously. APJ Abdul Kalam has paid tribute to his guru in the following words : "My relationship with Vikram Sarabhai was a deeply emotional and intellectual one. Time and again he placed his faith in me to lead teams that would design and develop mechanisms to take India further and further on her course to becoming a self- reliant nation, in terms of science and defence. He was a giant among men, and I was fortunate that that I could grow in his shadow. "

In his book, " My Journey : Transforming Dreams into Actions " APJ has devoted a chapter to Vikram Sarabhai, entitled "My Mentor : Dr Vikram Sarabhai". Here he has listed four leadership qualities of Dr Sarabhai : (1) Ready to Listen : (2) Ability to think Creatively (3) Ability to Build Teams (4) To look beyond failures. The book and the Chapter deserve every body's attention as much as Vikram Sarabhai's glorious life and work.

On India going to space, Sarabhai had famously said: "We are convinced that if we are to play a meaningful role nationally and in the comity of nations, we must be second to none in the application of advanced technologies to the real problems of the man and society." This must resound in the ears of every Indian, especially that of the policy makers.

A Resilient Boy Who Turned Adversity Into Opportunity!

Necessity is the mother of invention, so goes a proverb. Some have paraphrased it a little saying that 'Adversity' is the father of re-invention. The paraphrased statement may find justification in the life of Thomas Edison, one of the greatest innovators in history who struggled with adversity.

Thomas Alva Edison undoubtedly is one of the greatest of history who has contributed a lot to science and its applications. His inventions made in the later part of the 19th century have a major effect in our lives today. With persistent effort, he developed many devices that greatly influenced life in the twentieth century and beyond. Popular work of his includes the invention of light bulb, the phonograph, the motion picture camera, as well as improving the telegraph and telephone.

Edison was born to Sam and Nancy on February 11, 1847, Ohio, USA. He was poor in health in his childhood and poor in studies. Edison had started school late because of an illness. Three months later, he was removed from

school, a schoolmaster calling Edison "addled." His mother bestowed all love on the young kid and encouraged and taught him at home. He recalled later, "My mother was the making of me. She was so true, so sure of me; and I felt I had something to live for, someone I must not disappoint." His belief in self-improvement remained throughout his life.

Edison at the age of twelve, partially lost hearing capability. There are several theories regarding the loss of his hearing, one of them believed that it was the after effects of scarlet fever which he had as a child. While another theory says it was on a conductor boxing his ears after Edison caused a fire in the baggage car, an incident which Edison claimed never happened. Edison himself had a theory regarding his deafness that there was such an incident where he was lifted in a train by someone grabbing of his ears. But he did not let this disability to stand on his way. He treated the shortcoming as an asset, as it made it easier for him to concentrate on his experiments and research staying at home or lab. It needs no mention that his deafness made him alone and shy in dealing with others. Hearing impairment drove him to read more and more.

Thomas Edison when young was a hardworking enterprising man with high degree of determination and perseverance. He sold vegetables, candy and newspaper in trains. One day he saved a child from runaway train. The child's father repaid him by training him in operating telegraph. As a telegraph operator Thomas became interested in communications, which would be the epicentre of many of his inventions later.

He built his research work in Menlo Park, New Jersey. It was the first place where the only purpose was to invent. First there would be research and analysis, and then it would be implemented practically in a larger scale. There were lot of people working in this place who were tasked to invent and who would practically implement Edison's idea into invention. He founded more than one hundred companies and employed thousands of engineers, researchers, etc. He was the first inventors to apply the principles of mass production to the process of invention. At the time of his death, according to some estimate 15 billion US dollars of the national economy derived from his innovations alone.

The major inventions of Edison were the Phonograph, the Light Bulb and the Motion Picture camera. The phonograph was the first major invention by Edison which made him famous. It was the first instrument which was able to record sound and play it. Light bulb, although he did not invent the first electric bulb, but he made the first electric bulb that could be used in households (we may call it re-invention), he also invented the motion picture cameras that helped in moving forward the progress of movies. To his credit, he holds 1093 patents. Interestingly his first two kids had the nickname of Dot and Dash.

There are many virtues or qualities we all can learn from Thomas Edison: having perseverance, working hard and using time wisely. If we learn and apply these qualities in our personal life and in our business life, we will be able to accomplish our goals and become more successful.

Edison was an extraordinary talented inventor whose creativity improved the quality of life for billions of people. His resolve was to take responsibility for practical matters more than spending time in theorizing. There are many lessons to be drawn from his life. One, the mother is the best mentor and words of encouragement can do wonder. Two, one can turn adversity into opportunity with true determination. Three, failure is the pillar of success.

A few failures need not deter one from making another attempt and still another. Edison is believed to have failed myriad times- some put it at a thousand, while some say he failed ten thousand times - before finally being crowned with success in creating the light bulb, or developing the filament that would glow with current and hold it longer.

Importance of perseverance is made clear by Edison in this quote: "Our greatest weakness lies in giving up. The most certain way to succeed is always to try just one more time." Against all odds, Edison's mantra was perseverance, try one more time. If Edison did not always try one more time, he would not have invented the light bulb! People discouraged him saying that it will never work, but he didn't listen to those negative minded people. He believed that if he persevered through it, he would see light at the end of the tunnel, and he did. So, we have light to dispel the darkness of the night.

A Man of the Earth

These days when we get the news of forests burning or fire in the forests, what fires our imagination is about the man of the Earth. In recent years we have seen fires playing havoc in the forests of California in the US to that in forests of Australia and India being no exception. Unfortunately, Odisha lost large tract of forest cover due to fire recently and some miscreants causing fire were arrested by the police. It is reported that though there may be natural causes for the forest fires, some of these infernos happen due to wilful human intervention, or in other words due to the selfish interest of the timber mafia.

The timber mafias were also active then, when in the 1970s there emerged a Gandhian to be later known as a man of the earth, who saved the trees by leading a movement mainly involving ordinary women, the women of earth in their own rights who otherwise worship the earth, worship the trees and worship the nature in their distinctive ways. The man of earth besides leading the movement, created a consciousness about environment and the importance of the trees and forest in that. The movement as all school children would know is the Chipko movement something

unique in the history of social movements in human history.

Absolutely, we must remember Sunder Lal Bahuguna every day, especially when our forests are on fire and trees are being burnt. He was the main protagonist of the Chipko movement in the northern part of India. Chipko movement was a revolutionary, pioneering movement in a peaceful way to save the trees in India. Chipko, the Hindi word stands for hugging. It was an organized resistance to the destruction of forests spread throughout India. Thus, the name of the movement comes from the word 'embrace', as the villagers hugged the trees, and prevented the contractors' from felling them.

Sunder Lal was known as the person who educated Indians to hug trees to protect the them the environment by that. A catastrophic flood in Uttarakhand in 1970 made the people there to wake up to understand about the links between deforestation and the floods. Bahuguna led the Chipko movement from front and called for more people to join this campaign. As a result, many men and women in the Himalayas responded to his call for the protection of the environment, and formed a human chain around the trees to stop the loggers from cutting down the trees which they were doing on a routine basis, unhindered and in a massive scale. The tree huggers sent a strong message to the tree-fellers "Our bodies before the trees." The hug-the-tree movement also brought to world's notice the environmental crisis in the world's highest mountainous region.

Bahuguna whose childhood was spent in the Himalayas depicted that deforestation not only makes the place vulnerable for calamities, but it also leads to soil erosion and loss of fertility as a result of which many men in those areas are forced to leave the villages for the city or urban areas for their livelihood and earning. As a result of this migration of male folks to urban centres, their women are left behind alone with children and all responsibilities of collecting fodder, firewood and water. The Chipko movement became a catalyst in the fight to secure women rights. Many women joined in this fight and became an integral part of the movement, they tied rakhis (rakhi is a symbolic thread tied around the brother's wrist on the occasion of Raksha bandhan by a sister). Women worked with purpose and strong determination risking their lives to save the forests. They took away the cutting tools from the loggers in their endeavour to stop the cutting of trees. That again talks volumes about the courage of our village or forest-dwelling women and that of their mentor and leader Sunder Lalji!

Slowly this movement gained momentum and now the youth also seeing the cause and importance of women's save-tree actions, joined the Chipko Movement. Many college students along with women and other men staged peaceful demonstrations, did fasting and hugged trees. Bahuguna the chief architect of this Chipko movement with his flowing beard and trademark bandana (piece of cloth tied in head) went from strength to strength. There was a fasting in 1981 for Chipko movement and it yielded positive impact. There was a 15 year ban on commercial cutting of trees. Two years later Bahugunaji marched 4000 km in Himalayas to draw the national and global attention regarding environmental degradation.

Sunder Lal Bahuguna was a relentless fighter who kept on lecturing, educating about environment and leading rallies against deforestation caused by contractors abetted by forest officials. His heroic work and tunnel vision brought the movement to the notice of the then Prime Minister of India, Mrs Indra Gandhi. When Prime Minister Gandhi was asked about Chipko Movement, she said: "Well, frankly, I don't know all the aims of the movement. But if it is that trees should not be cut, I'm all for it."

Even after so many years, the relevance of Bahuguna's work is still well and truly alive. In 2017, social activists hugged around three thousand trees to stop them from getting cut to make way for Metro railway passage in Mumbai. Sunder Lal was a non-political, soft spoken person who understood the impacts of deforestation out of his own lived experience. He was very charismatic and a man of Gandhian principles. Sunder Lal believed in self-reliance and propagated it (now what PM Modi calls as 'Atma Nirbhar' meaning self-reliant). He like Gandhi believed in simple living and didn't like wasteful materialism. He said that India needed to produce biogas from human and animal waste, harvest solar and wind energy and hydro power from the run of the river. Bahuguna called for Improved Machines and Technology so that there is less consumption of energy to make India an energy secured nation permanently in a non-conflict and non-violence way. Sunder Lal died recently due to covid but he will be forever remembered as the man of earth, who did hard work all his life to protect and save the environment.

The Vaikom Movement

Long back, nearly 130 years ago, Swami Vivekananda had called Kerala a lunatic asylum as there was so much of dehumanising discrimination among people on the basis of caste. The lower caste people, particularly the so called untouchables, were not allowed to enter temples nor permitted to walk on roads adjoining places of Hindu God's worship. In 1924-25 the Vaikom Satyagraha was held which cited how independence from regressive social practices was important before fighting for the independence from the British. This movement is said to have made Kerala a progressive state giving dignity to all individuals without discrimination. (It is said that the people of Kerala, who could take in Vivekananda's caustic criticism with an open mind and in the right spirit, made use of the 'lunatic asylum' observation as an opportunity and inspiration for introspection and self-evaluation.)

The story relates to the Vaikom temple of Travancore and T K Madhavan, the great social reformer. Travancore was a princely state under British suzerainty. The Kingdom of Travancore was ruled by the Travancore Royal Family from 1729 to 1949 AD from Padmanabhapuram,

and later Thiruvananthapuram. At its zenith, the kingdom covered most of the south of modern-day Kerala and the southernmost part of modern-day Tamil Nadu. (The Vaikom Mahadev temple is now in Kottayam district of Kerala)

During this period, the early 20th century, caste discrimination and untouchability was rampant across India. Some of the most rigid and dehumanising norms prevailed in Travancore. Ezhavas and Pulayas were the lower castes who were considered polluting. Various rules were in place to distance them from upper caste Hindus. These included preventing people from, not just only on temple entry, but even on walking on the roads surrounding temples.

While the pernicious caste system was not unique to Travancore, some of the most rigid and ruthless inhibiting social norms and customs were prevalent there. Significantly the idea of caste pollution worked not only on the basis of touch but also sight. As a Portuguese traveller Duarte Barbosa wrote in his memoirs, "When (upper caste Nairs) walk along a street, they shout to the low caste folk to get out of their way ... this they do and if one will not, the Nayre may kill him."

TK Madhavan is said to be the architect of the Vaikom

Satyagraha. As the editor of Deshabhimani, a Malayalam newspaper, he raised the issue of social discrimination and injustice in that paper first. He moved a resolution in the state legislative council of Travancore in 1918 for ending the discrimination for which he received severe backlash from upper higher classes of Hindu community in the council.

He was able to move the petition after 5 years to a bigger platform in the Kakinada session of the Indian National Congress in 1923, a resolution for the eradication of untouchability.

It is widely acknowledged that T. K Madhavan's influence forced Gandhiji and Indian National Congress to include the abolition of untouchability in their national agenda. Madhavan had participated in that Kakinada Session of the Indian National Congress and moved a resolution for the eradication of untouchability with the support of Jawaharlal Nehru in 1923. He became a prominent leader of Sree Narayana Darma Paripalana (SNDP) Yogam which was formed for social reform among the Ezhava community.

This gained a nationwide support and formed a committee which was chaired by K Kelappan. It had people from different societies and had strong members like TK Madhavan, Kesava Menon, Velayudha Menon, K Neelakantan Namboothiri and TR Krishnaswami Iyer. All of them laid the foundation for Kerala Paryatanam movement in February 1924, which aimed that temple should allow entry to people of all castes and creed, as well as public road can also be used irrespective of one's social background.

It needs to be mentioned that T K Madhavan had got active support from Gandhiji in 1921 during a brief meeting held in Tirunelveli. Gandhiji had suggested that instead of demanding temple entry they should rather focus on access to wells and schools and later can take up the temple issue. But after discussion with Madhavan, Gandhiji said that Kerala was ripe for a temple entry agitation. To start the movement, the committee thought of putting all its attentions and effort on the Mahadeva Temple in Vaikom first, because of its Temple board had extremely strict rules regarding entry for lower castes. The oppressed caste tried to enter the temple in batches of three, but resulted in arrest by the police of Travancore.

On March 30, 1924, the Satyagrahis walked in procession towards the forbidden public roads. They were stopped fifty yards away from the place where a board cautioning the oppressed communities against walking on the road surrounding the Vaikom Mahadeva temple, was placed. Dressed in Khadi, Govinda Panikkar (Nair), Bahuleyan (Ezhava) and Kunjappu (Pulaya),defied the prohibitionary orders and attempted walking on the road. Stopped by police, in protest, the three men sat on the road and were arrested. Then, every following day, three volunteers from three different communities were sent to walk on the prohibited roads.

Gandhiji, Chattampi Swamikal and Sree Narayana Guru had backed this effort sincerely and the persistence and the continuous effort of the members of the Vaikom Satyagraha, these movement gained momentum and support started coming from different parts of the country and from different religions also. Akalis also started supporting the movement and even made camps at Vaikom, ran langers for the Satyagrahis.

Still the upper communities refused to allow lower caste people to be allowed. The movement was paused for a bit on the advice of Gandhiji to open the door for discussion between the two parties, but it did not bring a fruitful result. The movement was renewed and came with stronger determination, this time the important members were arrested such as TK Madhavan the architect of this movement, Kesava Menon, the flag bearer of this satyagraha, EV Ramaswami Naicker, an important member who came from Tamil Nadu.

On Gandhiji suggestion, on 1st of October 1924, a group of people belonging to upper caste marched in a procession with a petition which had 25000 signatures for allowing entry of the temple for everyone. Led by Mannathu Padmanabhan Nair from Vaikom, the march initially began with approximately five hundred people. Along the way, several people joined in, and by the time the procession reached Thiruvananthapuram in November, the strength had increased to a whopping 5,000. The 609-day long movement left an ever-lasting impact on the society as the display of one of the most nonviolent struggles for the caste oppressed people but still there was no favourable result.

In 1925 Gandhiji negotiated with W.H. Pitt, then Police Commissioner of Travancore and a settlement was signed between Government and Gandhiji. The Government agreed to nullify the prohibiting orders passed in February 1924 and Gandhiji gave his consent to withdraw the Satyagraha. The Government opened roads on three sides to all public except the eastern one that was reserved for the Savarna's (higher castes) only. To the credit of this Vaikom movement, a decade later the historic Temple Entry Proclamation was passed that did away with the obnoxious ban on the entry of marginalised depressed castes into the temples of Travancore.

It was a landmark achievement for the lower caste for defeating the hierarchical caste oppression. Today also Vaikom Satyagraha is celebrated as an example of struggle for the lower caste in gaining independence from oppression before gaining the final Independence from the Britishers in 1947. It was the first organised nonviolence movement against the repressive social norms that should always be remembered. The contributions of the satyagrahis such as TK Madhavan, K Kelappan and Kesava Menon should be written in golden letters. Without this India would have been a different place. In today's time not getting allowed to a temple or not walk in a road would be difficult to understand and would be a violation of the Constitution and basic human rights.

The Vaikom Satyagraha (1924-25)was a great success story of Gandhian peaceful methods. The movement continued for over six hundred days, non-stop. It is remarkable that through social pressure, police crackdowns and even natural disaster, it continued for so many days unabated till Gandhi called for a halt to do negotiation as mentioned above. It witnessed women empowerment as large number of women participated in the movement. Though it was a movement for the elevation of the lower depressed castes, higher class people from different parts did also join the jatra (journey). The satyagraha saw previously unseen unity across caste lines. Interestingly big guns of non-Hindu communities also lent their support to the movement, like barrister George Joseph and Abdul Rahman Editor-in-Chief of Young India.

As the year 2024 marks the centenary of the Vaikom Satyagraha, Chief Ministers of Kerala and Tamil Nadu jointly inaugurated the centenary celebrations. It is heartening to see that T.K. Madhavan finds a place as an unsung hero in the Azadika Amrit Mahostav and G-20 portal of Government of India.

(Collected and pieced together from different sources)

A Solo Adventurer in the Seas & Oceans

There are people who leave lasting imprints on the sands of time, never to be erased by the vagaries of nature because of their adventurous indomitable spirit which forms a part of history for all time to come and continues to inspire youngsters to emulate such feats. One such person was Mihir Sen. Sen was the first Indian and Asian swimmer to conquer the English Channel from Dover to Calais in 1958. He was fourth fastest swimmer to do so, took 14 hours and 15 mins to cover.

Though Mihir's name would be a house hold name in India for his extraordinary achievement in swimming in the treacherous seas or oceans, many people would not know that as a young boy, he grew up in the millennium city Cuttack that gave birth to Netaji Subash Chandra Bose and another legend Biju Pattanik, among others.

It is said that Mihir Sen was born to a Bengali family on 16th October 1930 in Purila, West Bengal. He moved to Cuttack, Odisha at the age of eight because Cuttack had better schools and his mother had a big role in this internal migration. Mihir went on to graduate in law from Utkal University in Bhubaneswar. He wanted to travel to England to prepare himself for the bar but had monetary constraints. With the help of Biju Patnaik (to be later the Chief Minister of Odisha) in 1950, Mihir Sen was able to go to England for pursing his studies. In England, he was hired at the India House by the Indian High Commissioner Krishna Menon. He was called to the Bar at Lincoln's Inn in 1954.

Florence Chadwick inspired Sen's swimming career, the first American to cross the English Channel in 1950. Sen wanted to repeat this feat for his own country. He had started his swimming journey in Kathajodi river in Odisha but that was hardly any preparation for English Channel. He then enrolled himself in the YMCA, London to develop his skills and endurance. He had to prepare hard for the high tides a swimmer faces in the English Channel, learning to cope with ever-changing weather, potential storms, and other natural calamities, as well as avoiding jellyfish and other dangerous creatures in the water. In 1955 he tried his first attempt, but luck was not on his side and weather forced him to abandon it. Three years later he was better prepared and with the experience of previous failure, he coated his body with mustard oil and finally achieved the feat of swimming the English Channel in 1958. In the same year he was awarded the Padmashri by the then P.M. Jawaharlal Nehru.

Then he achieved the unique feat of swimming oceans of five different continents in a single calendar year (1966) for which his name was registered in the Guinness Book of world record. He got two awards following this feat: Padma Bhushan and Blitz Nehru Trophy in 1967. Sen needed 45000 to pay the Indian army to record his Palk Strait swim. Half of the money he raised from the private sponsors and the other half was provided by then Prime Minister Indira Gandhi. Mrs Gandhi also ordered the Indian Navy to give full support to Mr Sen as it was a matter of pride for our country. The oceans across five continents which Mihir Sen swam in 1966 were: Palk Strait on April 5-6, Strait of Gibraltar on August 24, Dardanelles on September 12, Bosphorus on September 21, Panama Canal on October 29-30.

He was a lawyer, swimmer, and a well-known businessman. His company became the largest silk exporter in the country in a short spell of time. In 1977, Mr Sen was invited to join the Communist Party by the veteran politician Jyoti Basu of West Bengal, but the former turned down the offer. He rather tried his luck in electoral waters as an independent candidate but here the political waters were trickier than that of the Seas and Oceans. He was a free spirit and believed in freedom, both in the market place and the political space, as a result, it is rumoured that Sen perhaps suffered in business when Mr Basu and his party came to power in West Bengal.

Mr Sen died in June 1997 from a combination of Alzheimer's and Parkinson's disease. It is regrettable that Mr. Sen may be a forgotten name in Indian sports today, but those who know him remember and acknowledge him as one of India's finest sportspersons. He brought glory to the country at a time when India was a young nation, having just gained independence from the British, and had limited opportunities to excel in any field due to minimal investment in the sports sector. His achievements in such a context are truly spectacular and will always be written in golden letters in the annals of achievers and adventurers.

The Man who Became the First to Set Foot on Top of the World!

"One small step for a man, one giant leap for mankind", Neil A. Armstrong the first human to have put foot on the surface of Moon is known to have uttered these words. Armstrong was the Commander of the Spaceship Apollo 11 that landed there on 20 July 1969. Two other astronauts with him in the same mission were Buzz Aldrin and Michael Collins. Collins had remained in the Moon's orbit in the Command Module while Armstrong and Aldrin had taken the Lunar Module separating from the Space ship for landing. But everybody remembers Armstrong for being first as the "man on the moon" or as first human to do the moonwalk. Aldrin was less fortunate being seconds behind to put his feet on the moon.

The same could be said about Edmond Hillary the star of our story here. He was the first person to achieve a feat in another great adventure on earth and human history, the first person to put his foot on the top of the Earth- that is on the tallest peak of the Earth, the Everest in the Himalayas.

He is known as the first person to have conquered Everest, the highest peak.

Edmund Hillary was the first climber along with Tengzing Norgay to reach the summit of Mount Everest on 29 May 1953. News of their historic achievement, the world came to know a couple of days later, i.e., on the morning of June 2, the day of Queen Elizabeth II's coronation, Britons hailed it as a good omen for their country's future. Edmund Hillary belonged to New Zealand, a Commonwealth country, while Tenzing Norgay was a Sherpa of Nepal. They became the first known explorers to reach the summit of Mount Everest, which at 29,035 feet above sea level is the highest point on earth. But people remember Hillary, in the logic of being the 'first' one in anything, than they do remember Norgay. During past few days, major newspapers of the world are recounting the story of this historic feat throwing light on the man and the spirit that was Edmund Hillary celebrating the 70th year of that adventure.

Hillary was born on 20th July 1919 in Auckland, New Zealand which I had the opportunity of visiting recently. New Zealand is Nature and full of hills and mountains. It is said that Hillary was initially smaller in height than his classmates in school. Later he grew to be six feet two inches. It is said that in his young days he was shy but after taking up boxing he became confident. When he was 16 years old, he had been to a school picnic where he became interested in climbing and wanted to venture into tough world.

The world's highest point expedition in 1953 was done by Himalayan Committee which constituted Royal Geographical Society and the Alpine Club, in partnership with Times of London who sponsored half of the expedition expense in return for their press coverage. There was going to be separate attempts one by Charles Evans and

Tom Bourdillon, and then by Hillary and Tengzing who were part of the ninth British expedition to Everest led by John Hunt. The former team reached the south summit but was unable to achieve the highest point peak as they faced oxygen issues and were forced back 300m from the climax. Then came the turn of Hillary and Tengzing. It is said that the night before their climb the temperature was unbelievably low -34 degree Celsius with hurricane force winds which Tengzing gave a metaphor that "it sounded like the roar of thousand tigers."

It was at 11.30am on 29 May 1953 Hillary and Tengzing made history reaching the summit at 29,035 feet. Soon Tengzing raised the flags of the United Nations, UK, Nepal and India. He recited a prayer of thanks to Chomolungma, the more poetic name his people give to Everest, meaning "Goddess Mother of the World." In the snow he buried offerings, including sweets from his daughter to the Buddhist deities, while Hillary buried a crucifix given to him. They spent 15 minutes on the summit before starting their descend.

Although the pioneers had been a New Zealander and a Nepalese, the expedition was British. In the photograph taken at the summit, the British, Nepalese, Indian and United Nations flags flutter, but Hillary's & #39;s native country went unrepresented. That created a furore in New Zealand. Despite both of them being successful in climbing this summit and achieving this rare feat still one irritating question existed in the mind of the people who were too interested in general knowledge and trivial stuff, that who really reached the summit first? Tenzing said that over the decades there was "a lot of nonsense" talked about the subject and in his opinion, this was a lame question and rather people should celebrate the success of these climbers reaching the top in the face of such hostile and challenging weather and dangerous slippery conditions. The two climbers then had signed a joint statement saying both reached the summit almost together. The word "almost" did not satisfy the press and they asked: what exactly does "almost" mean? The men had been tied together by a 30ft rope, known to mountaineers as the "brotherhood of the rope." Tenzing held the loops which meant they were separated by about six feet. It is said that he was under tremendous pressure in India and Nepal to say that he himself was the first to reach. But in fact, it was Hillary, although only by a few seconds as he was leading that day. Hillary being a modest man resisted saying so, for much of his life. As reported, on reaching the summit of Everest, Hillary initially went to shake hands gracefully with Tenzing before the Sherpa threw his arms around him and slapped him on the back. Extremely excited, he said in an interview, "I did jump around, but I had a pretty strong feeling of satisfaction. It was a very good moment in that sense." But irrespective of this who reached first claim there remained a very warm relationship between the two Everest conquerors. Hillary was in complete awe of Nepal and set up the Himalayan Trust, a charity for the Sherpas. The trust built many hospitals, health clinics and more than thirty schools in the subsequent years, bringing support to the needy of that country. As for Tenzing, he never climbed Everest again. His final years he was in depression and isolation and he died in 1986 aged seventy-two. While Hillary served as New Zealand High Commissioner to India and Bangladesh and concurrently as Ambassador to Nepal from 1985 to 1988. In 2000 Time magazine named Hillary and Tenzing as two of the one hundred most influential people of the 20th century. And throughout the decades Hillary's colourful if irreverent phrase to his fellow New

Zealander George Lowe, "We knocked the bastard off," has continued to resonate with mountaineers everywhere. John Hunt, the British army colonel who led the 1953 expedition, is said to have refused to talk about the conquest of Everest. He rather only used the word the ascent - a concession to Tibetan reverence for Chomolungma, the goddess mother of the Earth. There was also speculation by some that George Mallory and Andrew "Sandy" Irvine in the 1924 British Expedition had perhaps made to the point of the summit from the Northern side. The Duo had no doubt come closer but disappeared during the summit attempt. After long 75 years of this attempt Mallory's body was found in 1999 frozen in ice by a mountaineer Conrad Anker. Irvine's fate is still shrouded in mystery. Whether Mallory and Irvine reached the summit before they died remains a subject of debate. In this sport ascent and descent, both are important. As Edmund himself put it, "If you climb a mountain for the first time and die on the descent, is it really a complete first ascent of the mountain? I'm rather inclined to think, personally, that maybe it's quite important, the getting down."

It may not be out of place to mention that most early attempts on Everest ascent were undertaken from the north (Tibetan) side. Chinese Revolution of 1949 and its subsequent annexation of Tibet led to the closure of that route. Climbers began to look at an approach from the Nepalese side. Hillary and Tenzing were the success stories of this route. At a recently held "Celebrating Everest 70" talk in Delhi organised by the Himalayan Environment Trust (HET) sons of the Himalayan heroes while paying tribute to their adventurous fathers revealed their concerns and approaches: Jamling Norgay : "My father provided me with good life and education. He told me after climbing

Photo taken in Auckland (May 2023, in Edmund Hillary's city)

Everest that he climbs so that I don't have to. This is the same thing that sherpas say to their children even today. Even recently, three sherpas died after falling into a deep crevasse on a dangerous section of Mount Everest." Jamling was thus highlighting how climbing is hazardous and the sherpa community is vulnerable and susceptible to risky livelihood due to the nature of their work Underlining the importance of cooperation and team work Peter Hillary said, "My family wanted me to become an engineer but I was drawn to what my father did…. ..We are so focused on the mountains and the challenge to climb them. But it is really about the people and cooperation I would like as many people to go to the mountains. I think this becomes more important now because we are all becoming urban creatures." Hillary remained humble despite so many honours and accolades, including British Knighthood, Diplomatic Caps, membership of the Order of New Zealand, honorary citizenship of Nepal, and a portrait on New Zealand's five-dollar note until his death in January 2008, at the age of eighty-eight. Let us end the story with Hillary's inspiring words, "Aim High! There is little virtue in easy victory"

An Encounter that Happened a Hundred Years Back

It was crossing of path between two laureates! In today's age, the crossing of path between two mutual admirers is no issue as it is dam easy since the communications and technology have developed in an unprecedented rapid stride. We have flights which make it faster to travel, and internet of course to connect people in a fraction of a second through the virtual path. But back then in early 1900s, there was very limited growth in commutation and technology. It becomes additionally more difficult for two people to connect when they both belong to different far-off countries in two continents cut off by seas and oceans. But when superior or divine force has desired to make it possible, it will happen anyhow.

Here we are talking about the crossing of paths between two global legends Rabindranath Tagore from India and Victoria Ocampo from Argentina. Victoria Ocampo was a writer, supporter of literature. In addition to contributing to Argentine literature, she extended her reach beyond her country, connecting with the cultural and

literary communities of Latin America, Europe, and the United States. Her admission to the Argentine Academy of Letters in 1977 marked a significant achievement, especially considering the challenges she faced as a young woman discouraged by patriarchal society from pursuing writing. Victoria established, financed, published, and edited a literary magazine called "Sur." This magazine showcased works from authors around the globe, featuring poetry, stories, essays, and social commentary. As a strong advocate for feminism, she was ahead of her time. Ocampo ended an unhappy marriage early in her life and lived independently thereafter. She was rumored to have numerous lovers, affairs, and friendships. Her travels took her across the globe, and she frequented artistic, literary, and social circles, particularly in France.

Ocampo encountered Tagore's work in 1914 when she read Gitanjali, describing it as having a profound impact on her youthful spirit. She likened Tagore's poetry to "magical mysticism," finding resonance in his portrayal of a loving and benevolent deity, which stood in stark contrast to the austere and punitive image of God from her upbringing. It was a dream come true, almost as if divine intervention had brought Ocampo and Tagore together to meet in person, allowing them to spend quality time.

Tagore, the global trotter, had to make a stop in Buenos Aires on November 6, 1924 for medical recuperation en route to Peru, where he intended to participate in the centenary celebrations of independence. Victoria Ocampo became aware of Tagore's situation and extended her offer to provide care for him. To accommodate his needs, she decided to utilize her assets, mortgaging her jewelry to secure a rental agreement for an elegant mansion located in San Isidro, a suburban area of Buenos Aires. Tagore resided there under her care, enjoying the scenic view from his balcony overlooking the expansive Plata River and the lush garden adorned with towering trees and vibrant flowerbeds.

During his stay, the 63-year-old Tagore is said to have experienced a rejuvenation under the attentive care of Victoria Ocampo, aged thirty-four at that point of time. Ocampo, displaying utmost devotion, attended to Tagore's needs and ignited his imagination. In turn, she found spiritual enlightenment and literary inspiration through her interactions with the esteemed Indian poet philosopher-. The pure affection Tagore held was met with reciprocal spiritual devotion from Ocampo. Following a complete recovery from his illness after a 58-day period, Tagore departed Buenos Aires on January 3, 1925. The face-to-face encounter between Tagore and Ocampo evolved into a significant cross-continental dialogue. Tagore expressed, "For me, the essence of Latin America will forever reside in your being." In response, Ocampo conveyed, "You are and will always represent India to me."

During his above 58-day stay as Ocampo's guest in Buenos Aires in that period, Tagore often sat in a comfortable armchair, his cherished one. Ocampo generously gave Tagore that armchair as a gift to take back to India from Buenos Aires. However, there arose a logistical challenge: the chair was too large to fit into Tagore's cabin aboard the ship. Undeterred, Ocampo, displaying her determined nature, instructed the ship's captain to widen the cabin door by breaking it down to accommodate the chair. Additionally, through her connections, Ocampo arranged for Tagore to have a specially designated two-bedroom cabin, a gesture that deeply impressed Tagore. Its significance remains to this day, as it is preserved at Shantiniketan, a testament to the enduring bond between Tagore and Ocampo.

During his final years, Tagore found solace in the same chair, where he would often relax and reflect. In April 1941, shortly before his passing later that year, Tagore even composed a poem inspired by the chair. Upon receiving news of Tagore's demise, Ocampo conveyed her condolences to Tagore's son through a simple yet poignant telegram stating, ‹Thinking of him' (pensando en el). It was this heartfelt sentiment that inspired the title of the Argentine movie. Pablo Cesar, the Argentine director and producer of this fascinating movie, amazed by this story has recreated the Tagore-Ocampo encounters based on the real-life story. This Indian Argentina connection is not known to many but it holds a real significance in the life of Tagore who was a great visionary for our nation India, and the author of our national anthem besides being that of Bangladesh.

Grape vines, rumor mills existed then as they do now. Tagore had become a global citizen after he wrote Gitanjali (1910) and his works had a profound impact on the intellectual movement in Latin America. How the small minds would understand higher minds and relationships that can be called deeply spiritual? True, they met each other very briefly in the 1920s, but their cross-continental ties continued through a series of letters that lasted till Tagore's death in 1941.

Let us remember that this spiritual encounter happened almost a hundred years back (November 1924). In this centenary year of that literary intercontinental connect, let me say my salutations to both Tagore and Ocampo!

(Published in Literary Vibes March 2024)

An Iconic Bridge

Bridges are platform or structure carrying the road which helps people to travel from one part to another through walking or through vehicles across a river or surmounting any other obstacle. But there are rare bridges which not only is meant for travelling but also has a historic importance for being great scientific achievement against odds and challenges, and again displaying aesthetic values, while serving as an iconic symbol for a nation. Here we are talking about the very popular Golden Gate Bridge of San Francisco, USA.

Golden Gate Bridge is a famous suspension bridge over the Pacific Ocean which links San Francisco city with Marin County of that country. The bridge construction started in 1933 and was finished in a record time of just four years in 1937.

The completion of the construction of the Golden bridge identified United States as a symbol of the power and achievement for the nation. At the time of its opening in 1937, it was both the longest and the tallest suspension bridge in the world, titles it held until 1964 and 1998, respectively. Its main span is 4,200 feet (1,280 m) and its

total height is 746 feet (227 m). It is a Pacific coast highway which is used for vehicular commutation. At the same time in the sideways it has pedestrian walkway. It was a significant engineering feat of its time, and it remains an iconic symbol of San Francisco and the United States.

On May 27, 1937, San Francisco's Golden Gate Bridge was opened to the public for the first time calling it as the "Pedestrian Day," that marked its opening... More than paying twenty-five cents each. The following day at noon President Franklin Roosevelt, from his far-off White House office, pressed a telegraph key and the Golden Gate Bridge was officially opened for vehicular use

The Golden Gate Bridge is described in Frommer's

(very popular American travel writer) travel guide as "possibly the most beautiful, certainly the most photographed, bridge in the world. The bridge's orange vermilion color, suggested by consulting architect Irving Morrow, has a dual function, both fitting in with the surrounding natural scenery and making it clearly visible to ships in fog. At night, the bridge is floodlit and shines with a golden luminescence that reflects off the waters of the bay and creates a magical effect. Despite its name, the bridge does not bear golden colour. Rather it is painted a reddish orange. This bright colour, called "international orange," often can be seen through the fog that forms over the bay for safe ship sailing.

Its construction, under the supervision of chief engineer Joseph B. Strauss, involved many challenges. It was an arduous task. The span of the bridge was more than twice that of any other bridge in the world. Workers had to blast away rock under deep water to plant the earthquake-proof towers. Other workers had to balance on cables high above the water. A movable safety net, innovated by Strauss, saved a total of as many as nineteen men from falling to their deaths during construction. But there had been casualty, a total of eleven worker lost their lives during the early phase of construction.

As pointed out above, Golden Gate Bridge is a suspension bridge. In this type of bridge, the roadway is suspended, or hung, from steel cables as one can see with the Howrah Bridge of Kolkata. The iconic Golden Gate Bridge features main cables suspended from two towers that emerge from the water. These towers stand at an impressive height of 746 feet (227 meters). Smaller cables extend vertically from the curving main cables, supporting the roadway. As a result, people have the opportunity to drive, bike, or walk across this historic bridge.

The Bridge, interestingly serves also as a political platform at times. Protests on even foreign policy issues have taken place on the bridge as it happened over the death of Mahsa Amini on September 26, 2022. Amini was the 22 year Iranian girl who had been taken into police custody for not wearing Hijab, the head-gown. Over 1,000 protesters had gathered at the Golden Gate Bridge's Welcome Center to demonstrate against the alleged human rights abuse in the Islamic Republic of Iran and its moral policing. The protest attendees voiced demands for women's rights and freedom. The event drew attention globally, sparking solidarity protests in Iran, Greece, England, and France.

I was fortunate enough to visit the Golden Gate Bridge this April in the first week. From my childhood I had harboured an interest to see the Golden Gate Bridge with naked eyes. I was studying in Homewood Middle School, at Birmingham, Alabama during 2007 -2008 but could not get the chance to travel to the West Coast and see this iconic marvel. After about 17 years I got the opportunity to see it on the sideline of my participation in the International Studies Association (ISA) 2024 Annual Convention. A modest travel grant helped me in this regard to see the wonderful city and the iconic bridge.

Overall, the Golden Gate Bridge is not only a vital transportation link but also a symbol of engineering prowess and a beloved icon of San Francisco and the United States and I feel truly blessed and lucky to witness the bridge.

Much like New York Harbor's Statue of Liberty, San Francisco's Golden Gate Bridge has achieved iconic status due to its breathtaking location and its association with the city. In May 1987, approximately 300,000 people participated in "Bridgewalk ‹87" to commemorate the bridge's fiftieth anniversary. Remarkably, two years later, during the 7.1-magnitude Loma Prieta earthquake on October 17, 1989, the elegantly suspended bridge remained unscathed.

It is truly a bridge that not only joins two parts of America, (San Francisco on one side and the Marin County on the other), but as large number of people from different parts of the world converge to see it, one may say that it bridges the world, the humanity at large.

(Published in Literary Vibes, April 2024)

Published in LV April 2024

An Iron Lady of India as an Inspiration to Everyone!

The Iron Lady we are talking of here is an extra-ordinary woman leader who took part in the Indian freedom struggle under the leadership of Mahatma Gandhi and made a mark in different fields which deserve to be recalled again and again. Durgabai Deshmukh (1909-1981), in addition to the tag of being a "freedom fighter", was a lawyer, educationist, politician and social activist who dedicated her life for the betterment of her country. It is not a matter of surprise that as with so many women in history, she remains largely unknown.

Born on July 15, 1909, in Rajahmundry, Andhra Pradesh, India to a conservative family, she was married at a very early age of eight to the son of a Zamindar. Traditionally, child brides would stay with their parents until they reached adulthood and then move to their in-laws' home. However, Durga defied these norms. By the time she came of age, she was already questioning societal conventions and contemplating reform. At the age of fifteen, she courageously walked out of her child marriage, having

discussed with her husband the wrongness of this practice. Her family's support played a crucial role in her decision."

In 1921, Durgabai made her presence felt. Upon learning that Mahatma Gandhi was scheduled to visit Kakinada in Andhra Pradesh for a political town hall meeting, she approached the organizers. Durgabai requested that Gandhi should spare some time to address a gathering of devadasis (temple dancers) and other women of marginalised sections. Her intention was for Gandhiji to discuss about social reform with them.

In a light-hearted challenge, the organizers told Durgabai jocularly that if she could raise Rupees 5,000 as present to Gandhi, she could have ten minutes' audience with him. Undeterred, she managed to collect the impressive amount within a week. However, when she approached the organizers, they claimed Gandhi had no time to spare. Durgabai persisted, and they eventually relented and honoured their promise. The event took place in her school compound, where Gandhi addressed an audience of women for over half an hour. Durgabai stood by his side, translating his speech into Telugu for those who did not understand Hindi.

Gandhi was so impressed with her that he asked her to accompany him as interpreter for the rest of his tour in the Andhra region. This was the peak of India's Non-

Cooperation Movement against the British and her actions could have led to arrest and imprisonment. That didn't deter Durgabai. In fact, it set the tone for what would be the first of many campaigns with the Congress and the freedom movement. In this context, the courage and conviction of a girl who was hardly twelve or thirteen by this time deserve any body's appreciation.

After the initial campaign, Durgabai, fuelled by national spirit, returned home and made a bold decision. She quit school to protest the colonial practice of imposing English-medium education. Instead, she founded the Balika Hindi Paathshala (Girls' Hindi School) to promote Hindi education for girls. Remarkably, a girl who should have been attending school herself was already running one.

Another interesting thing happened during this time which would throw light on her personality. She was volunteering in the Indian National Congress conference in 1923, where she didn't allow Jawaharlal Neha from entering the meeting as he did not have a ticket. Nehru was only allowed after he got the ticket, while seniors of Durgabhai were perplexed but Nehru appreciated her work.

She religiously took part in India's freedom movements like Salt Satyagraha, where she played a big role in mobilizing women to participate in the movement. She was imprisoned three times between 1930 and 1933. While in jail she self-educated herself in the subject of English. But here she saw the plight of women prisoners who even did not know why they were behind bars.

After her release from prison, Durgabai resolved to study law. Her goal was to provide free legal aid to those unjustly imprisoned and help them defend their rights. To pursue higher education, she applied to Andhra University. But an interesting thing happened again. The

Vice-chancellor hesitated to grant her admission due to the lack of a women's hostel. Undeterred, Durgabai took an unconventional approach.

In her autobiography, she recounts, 'I placed a newspaper advertisement inviting women who aspired to join Andhra University but faced hostel challenges to contact me. The response was positive. Ten of us came together, identified suitable premises, and established a hostel.'" Durgabai's determination and innovative thinking led to the creation of a women's hostel, enabling her and others to pursue education despite obstacles.

Durgabai earned her Bachelor's and Master's degrees in Political Science from Andhra University and later obtained a Law degree from Madras University. By 1942, she had established herself as a renowned criminal lawyer, practising at Madras Bar.

In the meantime, in 1937, she had founded the Andhra Mahila Sabha in Chennai (Madras) with the aim of promoting women's education and social welfare. This institution has grown over the years and continues to provide various educational and healthcare services. Durgabai was a strong advocate for women's rights and worked towards the upliftment of women and children.

She was one of the fifteen women members of the Constituent Assembly for drafting the constitution. As the founding fathers framed the Constitution of India, Durgabai actively participated in debates on critical issues. She advocated for property rights for women under the Hindu Code Bill and emphasized the significance of an independent judiciary. Remarkably, Durgabai, in her autobiography, recounted having proposed around 750 amendments, both independently and in collaboration with other Assembly members.

After independence, as the first woman member of the planning commission; Durgabai was responsible for the social welfare planning in the first five-year plan of the country. She was the first chairperson of the Central Social Welfare Board, established in 1953, which aimed to promote voluntary social work and support welfare organizations across the country.

In 1953, she married the then Finance Minister of India Chintaman Deshmukh. According to her own account, Prime Minister Jawaharlal Nehru was one of the three witnesses.

In 1963, Durgabai was appointed as a member of the Indian delegation to the World Food Congress in Washington DC. Subsequently, in 1965, she received an invitation from UNESCO to contribute to the preparation of a draft Asian Model for educational purposes. UNESCO recognized her significant contributions in the field of literacy and honoured her for her work."

Durgabai Deshmukh received several awards and honors for her contributions, including the Padma Vibhushan, India's second-highest civilian award, in 1975. She was an author and wrote several books and articles on social issues and her experiences. Deshmukh authored a book called The Stone That Speaketh. Her autobiography "Chintaman and I" was published one year before her death.

Durgabai Deshmukh passed away on May 9, 1981 leaving a remarkable rich legacy behind. Her ideas and work will stand strong among Indians for a long time to come. She is an inspiration to all, not just women. Her tireless efforts in promoting social justice, women's rights, and education have left an indelible imprint. Her life would continue to inspire generations of social workers, educators, and activists in India. Institutions she founded, such as the Andhra Mahila Sabha, remain active and continue to contribute to society. Her life and the impact she made serve as evidence of her unwavering dedication to improving society and her strong adherence to the principles of equality and justice.

(Published in Literary Vibes May 2024)

A Revolution and the Symbolic Role of Flowers

The revolution we are talking of here, happened fifty years ago in Portugal known as the Carnation Revolution. April 25, 1974 is that red letter day which not only marked freedom for its people, but freedom for the people of its colonies, ending the Portugal's colonial empire too.

The Carnation revolution was named after the carnations (a type of flower in Portugal) which were placed in the muzzle of the guns and uniforms of the soldiers as appreciation of their roles during the uprising. It was a bloodless coup led by the young military officers that resulted in the overthrow of the Estado Novo regime, a dictatorial government that had been in power since 1933 in Portugal. There were economic issues that had pinched the people. Portugal was one of the poorest countries of Europe at that time due to its colonial rule in many parts of the world. That the desire for democracy among the common people were at the heart of this revolution. The Carnation Revolution's commitment to ending colonialism can be seen as part of the same historical wave that had influenced Goa's liberation in 1961. Although Goa was liberated more than a decade earlier, the Carnation revolution, one may say, had reinforced the global trend towards decolonization and self-determination.

We will recall that on December 19, 1961, India annexed Goa in a swift military operation, after years of diplomatic efforts to secure its independence from Portugal had failed. Though the Government of India under Nehru had been trying all possible diplomatic and peaceful means to see Portugal's withdrawal from Goa, the dictator of Portugal, Antonio de Oliveira Salazar, was too adamant to yield. In fact, he had gone a step further to declare the Indian territories under Portuguese rule were not colonies, but overseas provinces, integral parts of 'metropolitan Portugal.' Portugal by this time had joined the NATO (North Atlantic Treaty Organisation), and Salazar demanded that any military action by India be met with a NATO response.

Coming back to the Carnation Revolution, three African countries that got Independence for this revolution were Angola, Mozambique, and Guinea-Bissau. Portuguese rule in Africa was characterized by the exploitation of African people and resources. Decolonization after World War II had put immense pressure on countries like Portugal who were colonial powers to grant independence to their colonies. Portugal's conflicts with its colony led to high financial loss. The sheer cost of the bloody colonial war that Portugal's government insisted on fighting from 1961 – principally in its colonies mentioned above – took its toll. By the eve of the revolution 13 years later, nearly 40% of the national budget had been spent on fighting the war, and nearly every family had been impacted, with a brother, son, father, uncle, or cousin conscripted.

Especially young military officers were unhappy and dissatisfied for the unpopular wars and unnecessary shedding of bloods in foreign soils. They rightly felt that this was draining the country's resources. The young officers were the flag bearers of this revolution. With them University students and intellectuals were at the forefront of opposition to the regime, organizing protests.

This Carnation Revolution in Portugal marked a pivotal moment in the nation's history. On this transformative day, the Salazar dictatorship not only came to an end, but as already stated, five centuries of colonization. Antonio de Oliveira Salazar, the Portuguese dictator, had passed away earlier, in 1970. His regime, known as Estado Novo, had endured for over four decades, leaving an indelible impact on the country—a symbol of oppression, inequality, and unfreedom.

The Carnation Revolution, characterized by its peaceful uprising, liberated Portugal from tyranny and set the stage for a new era of freedom and change, paving the way for Portugal's transition to democracy. It was a turning point that resonated deeply with the people, forever altering the course of their nation's destiny. To this day, April 25 is celebrated as a national holiday in Portugal as Freedom Day. Following the Carnation Revolution, the carnation was officially declared Portugal's national flower in 1974.

The name "Carnation Revolution" itself comes from the fact that almost no shots were fired during the uprising. When the population took to the streets to celebrate the end of the dictatorship, the simple carnations offered to soldiers by a restaurant worker, Celeste Caeiro, became a powerful symbol of hope and change. To this day, the red carnation remains ingrained in national celebrations, memorials, and daily life. So yes, the carnation is not only a flower but also a living emblem of Portugal's remarkable journey toward liberty.

This year(2024) tens of thousands of people marched on the streets of Lisbon on the Freedom Day carrying Carnations, waving national flags and shouting: "April 25 – Always. Fascism Never Again! ".

In the spirit of those carnations, may hope and freedom continue to bloom.

(Published in Literary Vibes June 2024)

A Healing Statesman

There are many notable and talented physicians, famous politicians, founders of important associations, but rarely do we see a combination of all these three in one person. And add to that the person we are talking of was a freedom fighter and in post-independence India had made contributions for the planning and development of the mega cities like Durgapur, Kalyani, and Bidhannagar (Salt Lake City). Here we are talking about none other than the enigmatic Bidhan Chandra Roy. Affectionately known as "Doctor Da," Bidhan was more than a physician; he was a visionary statesman who left an indelible mark on the fabric of our nation.

Born in Patna in the year 1882, Bidhan's father, Prakash Chandra Roy who came from a wealthy family was serving as an excise inspector. His mother, Aghorkamini Devi, was religious and a devoted social worker. It is learnt that his mother had a key role in shaping Bidhan's personality. She taught him Bhagvad Gita and the writings of Rabindranath Tagore. Bidhan was the youngest of five siblings – he had two sisters and two brothers. Prakash Chandra, Bidhan's father was a descendant of the family of Maharaja Pradapaditya, the rebel Hindu king of Jessore (now in Bangladesh), but did not inherit much wealth from his ancestors.

He did his graduation in Mathematics from Patna college. Later he did his medical studies from University of Calcutta. While at medical school, Bidhan came upon an inscription which read, : "Whatever thy hands findeth to do, do it with thy might;" These words became a lifelong source of inspiration for him. Bidhan for his further studies left for Britain in February 1909 with, as it is said, Rs 1200 only in his pocket. The then dean of St. Bartholomew Hospital was reluctant to accept an Asian student. So, he rejected Bidhan's application. Roy submitted several additional applications till the Dean, after 30 admission requests, admitted Bidhan. He completed his studies in two years and three months. No surprise that this talented guy, became a member of the Royal College of Physicians (MRCP) and a fellow of the Royal College of Surgeons (FRCS) in May 1911. He also returned home after some months in the same year.

In his medical career he was immensely respected. He showed full dedication and hard work in health service. He even served as a nurse when needed. Besides that, he practiced privately, charging a nominal fee. He was personal physician to Mahatma Gandhi. He played a key role in establishing the Indian Medical Association and the Medical Council of India, also instrumental in the establishment of several medical colleges. He believed that freedom would remain a far dream till people are healthy and strong both physically and mentally.

He served as the Chief Minister of West Bengal from 1948 to 1962 an unprecedented 14 years. As pointed out above, his tenure transformed many cities such as Durgapur, Kalyani, and Bidhannagar (Salt Lake City) into urbanized cities with good infrastructures and facilities. For championing the cause of education, industrialization, and rural development, Dr. Roy is known as the "Architect of West Bengal's Renaissance." His vision transformed Calcutta (now Kolkata) into a hub of culture, education, and scientific progress. He was a member of Indian National Congress and actively participated in Indian Independence Movement. He had a key role in the establishment of several educational institutions, including the Indian Institute of Technology Kharagpur.

Dr. Bidhan Roy, renowned for his uncanny diagnostic powers, left a lasting legacy. One incident stands out: A few years before his death, he traveled to Vienna for an eye operation. As preparations for the surgery unfolded, he heard sounds of somebody coughing. His immediate demand — "Who coughed?" — startled the room.

The offender? A fellow doctor. Dr. Roy insisted on an X-ray, convinced the doctor had tuberculosis. Despite hesitation and scepticism, the junior doctor was X-rayed, and the diagnosis confirmed Dr. Roy's intuition. His fame had indeed reached Vienna, where even a cough didn't escape his diagnostic radar. Dr. Bidhan Roy's ability to perceive beyond the obvious remains an awe-inspiring tale in the annals of medicine.

A healer and leader, the renowned physician, Dr. Roy healed countless lives, beyond physical health, he also worked tirelessly to heal the social and economic disparities plaguing post-independent India. He was awarded the Bharat Ratna in the year 1961. July 1 is celebrated as National Doctor Day in his honour. Interestingly July 1 date was significant in his life, he was born and his demise was on the same date. After his death, his house became a nursing home named after his mother, Aghorkamini Devi. He had also constituted a trust for his properties at Patna to carry out social service. His legacy continues to inspire many in the fields of medicine and public service in India. The Dr. B.C. Roy National Award, conferred for excellence in various fields, stands as a testament to his enduring impact.

(Published in Literary Vibes July 2024)

Atomic Thoughts about the Little Boy and Fat Man !

Come the month of August, we rejoice on the thought of August 15, our Independence Day! But August also brings the thoughts of agony to many. There comes the memory of the Little Boy and Fat Man. The famous "An eye for an eye makes the whole world blind" by Mahatma Gandhi means if we punish people who we believe to be cruel, we become just as wicked and cruel as the people who we are punishing. We are now talking about the World War II cataclysmic events in its closing year when USA dropped two atomic bombs on Hiroshima and Nagasaki. Many experts argue that the atomic bombings were required to end the war with minimal casualties, ultimately preventing a greater loss of life. Conversely, critics contend that the bombings were unnecessary for concluding the war and the act constituted a war crime, raising significant moral and ethical concerns.

In the final year of second world war, the Allies were preparing for an invasion of Japanese mainland. This plan followed an extensive bombing campaign that severely damaged 64 Japanese cities. After Germany's surrender on May 8, 1945, which ended the war in Europe, the Allies focused their full attention on the Pacific War. By July 1945, the US, through the Manhattan Project, had developed two types of atomic bombs: Little Boy, a uranium-based weapon, and FatMan, a plutonium-based weapon. The United States Army Air Forces 509th Composite Group was trained and equipped with a specialized version of the Boeing B-29 Superfortress and stationed at Tinian in the Mariana Islands. On July 26, 1945, the Allies issued the Potsdam Declaration, demanding the unconditional surrender of Japan's armed forces, warning that failure to comply would result in prompt and utter destruction. The Japanese government disregarded this ultimatum.

The United Kingdom's consent was secured for the bombings, as mandated by the Quebec Agreement. On July 25, General Thomas Handy, the acting Chief of Staff of the United States Army, issued orders for atomic bombs to be deployed against Hiroshima, Kokura, Niigata, and Nagasaki. These cities were selected as targets due to their large urban populations and the presence of militarily significant facilities.

On that dreadful day of August 6 and 9, 1945 respectively, the United States dropped atomic bombs on the Japanese cities of Hiroshima and Nagasaki. These bombings resulted in the deaths of an estimated 150,000 to 246,000 people, the majority of whom were civilians. These events mark the only instances of nuclear weapons being used in warfare. Japan surrendered to the Allies on August 15, just six days after the Nagasaki bombing. The formal surrender was signed by the Japanese government on September 2, officially ending the war.

Many people say to prevent the atrocities carried

out by Japanese soldiers this was needed. But it had a huge impact. Nuclear weapons are the most destructive, inhumane, and indiscriminate weapons ever created. Both in the scale of the devastation they cause, and in their uniquely persistent, spreading genetically damaging radioactive fallout, they are unlike any other weapons. A single nuclear bomb detonated over a large city could kill millions of people. The use of tens or hundreds of nuclear bombs would disrupt the global climate, causing widespread famine. A single nuclear weapon can destroy a city and kill most of its people. Several nuclear explosions over modern cities would kill tens of millions of people. It hardly takes 10 seconds for the fireball from a nuclear explosion to reach its maximum size.

A nuclear explosion releases vast amounts of energy in the form of blast, heat and radiation. An enormous shockwave reaches speeds of many hundreds of kilometres an hour. The blast kills people close to ground zero, and causes lung injuries, ear damage and internal bleeding further away. People sustain injuries from collapsing buildings and flying objects. Thermal radiation is so intense that almost everything close to ground zero is vaporized. The extreme heat causes severe burns and ignites fires over a large area, which coalesce into a giant firestorm. Even people in underground shelters face likely death due to a lack of oxygen and carbon monoxide poisoning.

In the long-term, nuclear weapons produce ionizing radiation, which kills or sickens those exposed, contaminates the environment, and has long-term health consequences, including cancer and genetic damage. Their widespread use in atmospheric testing has caused grave long-term consequences. Physicians project that some 2.4 million people worldwide will eventually die from cancers due to atmospheric nuclear tests conducted between 1945 and 1980.

In today's time there is no room for the usage of nuclear bomb and conflicts should be solved through diplomatic talks. Nuclear weapons are the most destructive, inhumane, and indiscriminate weapons ever developed. Their unparalleled ability to cause widespread devastation, combined with the long-lasting, pervasive, and genetically harmful effects of radioactive fallout, sets them apart from all other weapons. A single nuclear bomb detonated over a major city could result in the deaths of millions. The deployment of tens or hundreds of such weapons would have catastrophic effects on the global climate, potentially leading to the destruction of the human race.

Albert Einstein had said, " Nuclear weapons have changed everything except our way of thinking, and thus we drift toward unparalleled catastrophe. " Today of course there is a widespread recognition that nuclear war would be highly dangerous than any conventional war. Today's nuclear weapons have far more destructive capacity than the Hiroshima and Nagasaki bombs. Nuclear war once unleashed will efface humanity from the Earth and should be avoided at any cost. These are but hanging on the humanity without their conscious knowledge. As Pandit Nehru said the right to life of the humanity has been taken away without their consent. There should be a worldwide demand for de-nuclearization and both declared and undeclared nuclear weapon states should give it up! But will it ever happen?"

(Literary Vibes 30 August 2024.)

Black Eagle Books

www.blackeaglebooks.org
info@blackeaglebooks.org

Black Eagle Books, an independent publisher, was founded as a nonprofit organization in April, 2019. It is our mission to connect and engage the Indian diaspora and the world at large with the best of works of world literature published on a collaborative platform, with special emphasis on foregrounding Contemporary Classics and New Writing.

www.ingramcontent.com/pod-product-compliance
Lightning Source LLC
Chambersburg PA
CBHW060608080526
44585CB00013B/733